Perpetual Motion

A Refugee Childhood

Perpetual Motion

A Refugee Childhood

Recalled and Illustrated

by

Renate Melinsky

This book is dedicated to the memory of
my parents

Larks Press

Published by the Larks Press
Ordnance Farmhouse, Guist Bottom, Dereham
Norfolk NR20 5PF
01328 829207
email: Larks.Press@btinternet.com

November 2004

Printed at the Lanceni Press
Garrood Drive, Fakenham

British Library Cataloguing-in-Publication Data
A catalogue record for this book is available
from the British Library.

Acknowledgement
I should like to record my gratitude to my husband,
Hugh, for his patience in checking my text and
suggesting improvements,
and for typing the final script.

ISBN 1 904006 24 8

..covered with duvets and blankets,...a woolly hat put on my head and was left to sweat it out.

Towers of open rolls revolving slowly

'You don't get a picture, you're Jewish...'

I had left my dog Tref behind in the last train. There was no going back.

...to practise on a length of cardboard

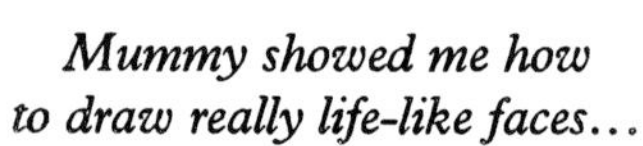

Mummy showed me how
to draw really life-like faces...

When no one was looking,
I spat them out into the sink.

CHAPTER ONE

Early Years: 1927–1935

I was born on the seventeenth of October, nineteen twenty-seven, in a beautiful dark brown mahogany bed which my mother later told me was Napoleon's. But eventually I realised that it was made in the style of the Emperor's bed. That was in Berlin at Number 45, Pariserstrasse. We lived in a very large *art nouveau* block which had eight huge flats in it built round a courtyard. Ours was on the fourth floor, up a wide flight of stone stairs. By the time I arrived it had been divided into two.

Tommy, my brother, was five years older than I and, until my arrival on the scene, was the apple of my parents' eyes, pretty, wearing 'Boy Blue' clothes, and very amusing and intelligent. My appearance spoilt his central position and he resented me, maybe because his request to my mother had not been answered. He had asked her before my imminent arrival, 'Could the baby have pink eyes, please?' Everyone was very relieved that mine turned out to be brownish green like my mother's and Tommy's. Daddy had very pale blue eyes behind glasses. My father did not like the look of me when I arrived and said I was '*Ein niedlicher kleiner miesnik*', (a dear little ugly wretch), because my nose resembled an electric socket. In those days sockets had two holes.

One of my earliest memories is of being pushed in a large pram and looking up into the hood. It was dark outside, but as we went along the gas-lit street, lamps lit up the inside of the hood for a brief moment, and then faded, and the next lamp would take over, lighting up the pram and then fading, and so on. I remember waiting for the next one, and the next. Maybe that is why years later in London I enjoyed the similar effect on my bedroom ceiling at night, only then it was car headlights, not lamp-posts, and they were moving and not I.

Our flat had a large drawing-room with a raised dais area by the bay window, where Daddy sat with his drawing board, set-square, T-square, slide-rule, pencils, rubbers, rolls of paper and other architectural necessities, designing houses, and later I stood watching him and had my first drawing lessons. The piano in the

drawing-room was seldom played but it was used for vases of flowers and Christmas and birthday presents. There was also a lovely glass-fronted cupboard in which the best porcelain was kept as well as a boat-shaped cut-glass container which always had home-made marmalade in it. I only remember the occasional spoonful, eaten on its own and never on bread.

After Christmas I used to keep the left-over dried figs in this cupboard. They had been arranged with other sweet-meats and *petits fours* on a large plate from which we were allowed to help ourselves when we wished: I only liked the figs stone-hard, when I would gnaw them to the disgust and amusement of the family.

The next room along the corridor was the dining-room which doubled up as Tommy's and my bedroom and playroom. In the corner by the window was a caged bullfinch who was fed on a weed we collected whose smell I can still recognise. Lina, our faithful cook, maid and nanny, used to put a white napkin over the cage at night so that he would go to sleep. My cot was in another corner by the door, and when I was a little older a beautiful white doll's pram stood next to it with a realistic baby doll inside. It also came in useful for my baby teeth as they came out one by one and were put on the hood for the tooth fairy to collect in exchange for a coin. A friend of Mummy's wore a silver brooch in the shape of a lily of the valley, but the flowers on it were made of the first milk-teeth of her five children.

In another corner I had a tiny table, chair and bench where my dolls sat. One was called Gaduina, a name I invented, and a boy one was called Hänschen, dressed in Tyrolean costume with a green pointed hat and *lederhosen*.

One day one of Mummy's many friends came to tea with one hand behind her back in a mysterious way. I guessed that she had a present for me, but she teased me terribly and I got quite angry. Eventually she showed me what she had brought – a doll's deck chair, exactly like a real one with a striped canvas seat. I was beside myself with delight, but I never forgave her for teasing me so much. Hänschen fitted into it exactly.

Near the bench was a wonderful dolls' flat made by my parents (for we all lived in flats in those days) as a birthday present. It had a tiny bathroom complete with wash-basin, bath and lavatory, and the taps could be turned on with water coming out, from a tank at the top of the flat. There was also a bedroom and kitchen. I was ecstatic when it was given to me.

Our dining table was in the centre of the room with a lamp hanging from the ceiling above it which could be pulled up or down at will. On the floor below lived Joachim Prausnitz whose father was a doctor, and when he came upstairs to play we used the lamp, pulled down, to X-ray my dolls. Tommy played with his trains on the floor.

At mealtimes Mummy sat with her back to the window, facing the door. When the first course was finished she would step on the bell hidden under the carpet and Lina would come and clear away, mumbling to herself, and then bring in the second course. She cooked delicious Austrian dishes, as both she and Mummy came from Vienna, in her spotless white kitchen. Its window looked out on to a yard a long way below, where she and the maids from the other flats hung out their washing, but it meant that she had to carry it down four flights of stairs and then up again. Lina lived in the kitchen. I never saw where she slept, but she cooked there, washed and ironed there, and in the evening she

sat in the dark to have her supper there with a tankard of beer. She preferred the dark to save my parents the cost of electricity. I often went to keep her company: she was my favourite person.

Outside the dining room window was a little balcony overlooking a green square with a Victorian red-brick church at the far end.

At the corner nearest our block was a public lavatory. Tommy and I used to stand on the balcony to watch the world go by, especially the people who used this *Knusperhäuschen,* as we called it, after the witch's house covered in gingerbread in Humperdinck's opera *Hänsel und Gretel.*

On St Nicholas' night, the sixth of December, all German children put one of their little boots between the windows of the double-glazing and when they woke up in the morning they found a *St Nikolaustüte,* that is a brightly coloured cone made of card into which St Nicholas had put tangerines and sweets and even small toys for the children who had been good all the year, but for the bad ones a lump of coal and a little black devil made from a fluffy pipe-cleaner.

My parents added a figure of St Nicholas made of dates, figs and raisins with clothes made from coloured paper and gold and silver foil, all supported by wooden skewers. He always had a mitre on his head and carried a crozier because he was a bishop. One night when St Nicholas was due, I stayed awake to have a look at him. The door opened very quietly and a figure stole into the room, but then another followed, and I saw that they were my parents tip-toeing in with two cones. End of myth.

For Christmas dinner we had a goose. Outside was thick snow on the balcony. The fat from the goose was poured into a big bowl with chopped livers mixed in, then Lina took it out, steaming, on to the balcony where it sank through the snow on to the floor.

Later, when the fat had solidified, she fetched it in, and it always left a most satisfying round black hole in the snow. We ate the goose-fat on bread with a sprinkling of salt. Delicious! Usually Tommy and I had a kind of jam called *Powidel* on our rolls for breakfast. Lina made this from dark pointed plums called *Zwetchken* which were boiled for ages until the wooden spoon made clear paths on the base of the pan. It was made without sugar but had a wonderful taste. We drank cocoa with our breakfast.

Then, of course, there was illness. When I was still quite small I developed boils, which I am told were all over my back and bottom. Dr Nathan, a children's specialist, hypnotised me and then lanced them, but I am happy to say that I remember nothing of this. I do remember later visiting his surgery where the waiting room, painted pink, was full of children with their mothers and many lovely toys to play with. There was also a real nurse with white cap and apron over a blue dress, and so I definitely wanted to be a nurse and in the meantime I needed the proper outfit for my birthday. My mother made the apron but bought the genuine head-dress from a shop. I was in my seventh heaven.

Later, whenever I started a cold, I was immediately immersed in a steaming hot bath till I was beetroot in colour, wrapped in hot bath towels, and rushed into bed, previously heated with numerous hot-water bottles. Then I was covered with duvets and blankets, and finally had a woolly hat put on my head, and was left to sweat it out. I had to drink boiled milk with honey in it, and I still hate the taste of boiled milk. When Daddy had an upset tummy, which was quite often, he would eat *Haferschleim*, a runny sort of porridge, and I heartily disliked seeing him spoon up that slimy grey concoction. When he had colds he used to treat them by breathing in steam from a bowl of boiling water with his head underneath a big towel. There was once such a bad flu epidemic that we were all infected so that we had to have a nurse to look after the family. She put glycerine on my lips to stop them cracking and asked me what I thought it was. When I said 'Sugar' she answered crossly, 'No, it isn't: it's glycerine'.

Tommy once developed warts on his hands caused by his having to eat raw eggshells because he was short of calcium. Crunch, crunch: no calcium tablets in those days. He was taken to a kind of doctor who made him promise never to tell anyone what treatment he had received. So Tommy promised and came home, never telling a soul, and in a little while the warts mysteriously vanished.

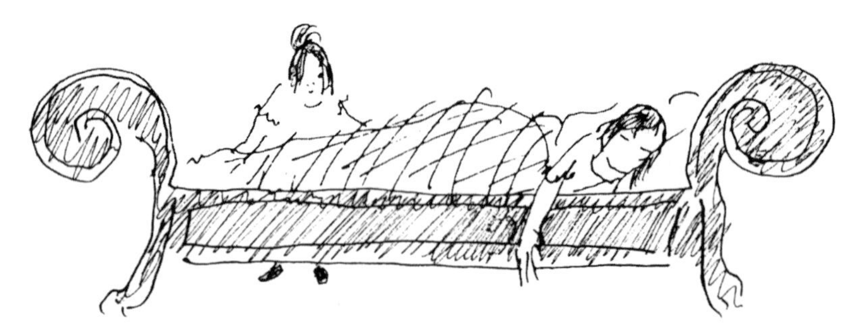

Mummy was ill once and lay in her huge Napoleonic bed looking white and with a very sore throat. The doctor said he would have to operate on it as she had an abscess, but Onkel Wipp, a close friend of the family, said, 'Her throat is far too beautiful to be cut open'. So instead she had to eat endless anchovies, which were very salty but did the trick. I enjoyed helping her eat these and still count them among my favourite foods.

When she was better, she showed me how to crochet so that I could make clothes for my dolls. We sat on the sofa and a little garment grew miraculously from a huge ball of pink wool, which we had wound from a skein. When the little jacket was finished we put an edging of white fluffy angora round the neck. Then we twiddled a pink cord from the wool and threaded it in and out of the garment's waist. Knitting came much later on and the first thing I ever made was most unsuitable for a beginner, but I was adamant. It was a pale grey skating skirt with several gores to make

it swirl. Needless to say, by the time it was finished I had decided that skating was not for me with my weak ankles.

When I was four I went to kindergarten, together with Joachim from downstairs. The two nice ladies who ran it were called Tante (Aunt) Ellen and her sister Tante Inge. We played lots of games, learned how to make interesting objects out of paper and performed graceful dances in pink floaty dresses: this was called 'Greek dancing' and was the latest craze. We performed a play for our parents about Chanuka, the Jewish equivalent of Christmas, in which seven little girls held candles, representing the Menorah, the seven-branched candlestick, and the oldest boy as a server lit our candles one by one.

That summer, it must have been nineteen thirty-two, the entire kindergarten went on holiday into the country. As it was very hot we were allowed to go about in pants only, and as a result I was nicknamed 'Gandhi' after the famous Indian politician who had long brown skinny legs like mine and wore only a white loin-cloth. Parents were asked not to visit, but Mummy did come in the second week, which gave me such a shock that I fell off the potty I was sitting on. After she left I became homesick and cried a lot. We were encouraged to wash and dress ourselves and do our own hair, but I could not manage my *bananentolle*, my banana-shaped topknot. Mummy did it with the greatest of ease, using a curved comb rolled into the hair until it touched my head and then pushed in firmly. Poor Tante Ellen tried so hard to do it but eventually gave up, sticking a single hair-slide into my hair to keep it out of my eyes.

For my next birthday there were as usual several traditions to be observed. The birthday girl had to stay in the dining-room while the rest of the family took their presents to the drawing-room where they were piled on to the piano round a beautifully arranged vase of my favourite flowers, pompom dahlias. When all was ready I was allowed in and showered with hugs, kisses and presents. Lunch followed with my favourite food, sauer-kraut and frankfurters with lots of brown mustard, and later my friends, mostly from the kindergarten, came for the party bringing their presents, and we played games until teatime. The centre-piece of this was a huge chocolate cake filled with *schlag* (sweetened whipped cream) and Morello cherries, topped with glistening chocolate icing. There were candles on top to be blown out later by me. My friend Marion adored the cake above all else and while still eating the first slice said, with her mouth very full, 'Can I have another slice, please?'

After tea Daddy performed his 'napkin nonsense', a hilarious interlude when, with a deadly serious expression on his face, he tried to roll up his huge white napkin and stuff it into the small napkin ring, and as he got it entangled with the table cloth or his tie everyone rolled about laughing. The next game was the Turk's Leg when all the children were sent out and one by one were introduced blindfold to the Turk, who was Mummy dressed up in eastern clothes with a turban on her head, sitting on a mound of cushions, and told to pull one of his legs off. If they chose the right one it came off in their hands – a stuffed one. We also played Nelson's Eye when a blindfolded child had to put a finger into damp bread and was told that it was Nelson's eye-socket.

My family over several generations had never been practising Jews, no sabbath services in synagogues or observance of festivals, but in 1933 they decided to celebrate Chanuka instead of Christmas. They prepared for it with advice from friends about special games to play, special ways of hiding presents, and special food. After the meal we played a game with sweets in bowls and a spinning top with Hebrew letters on it, but as we did not know any Hebrew we made up our own rules about giving and taking. After this, at last, we could open our presents, hidden under a white

נ Nun – nothing happens. – next player spins
ג GIMEL – take all sweets from all players
ה HEY – take half sweets " " "
ש SHIN – put 1 sweet into centre bowl

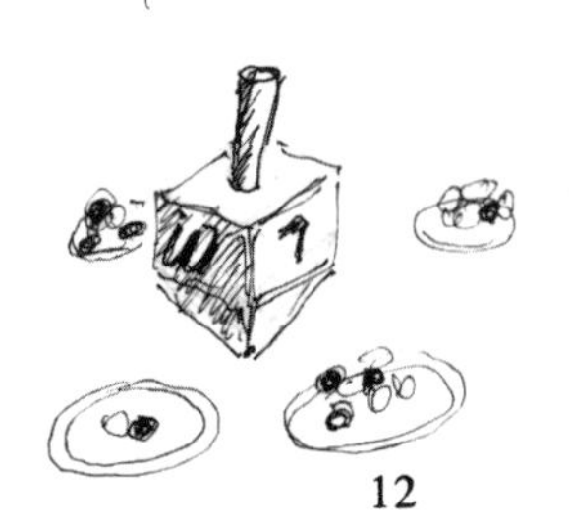

napkin on the piano. We liked Chanuka but begged to have Christmas as well because we missed the Christmas tree. Mummy proudly told friends how we had celebrated, listing the food we had eaten, including pork, hare and ham and they were much amused because these are forbidden to Jews.

Christmas was the only time when my mother was allowed into the kitchen by Lina in order to make *Weinachtsbäkerei,* traditional Christmas biscuits. She spent days crystallising fruit. This was a matter of cutting the chosen fruit into neat chunks, boiling them in sugar and then leaving them to dry overnight. This process was repeated several times and then they were threaded on to wooden skewers until they were needed. All this, of course, was of great interest for us children who were always at hand to lick bowls and spoons. Of a different sort were *Hazelnussbusserln,* hazel-nut kisses, topped with nuts dipped in egg-yolk to stop them falling off, *Pariserstangerln,* a kind of marzipan made with hazel nuts instead of almonds and coated with lemon icing, then hardened and cut into sticks as long as my finger, *Vanillebutter* made of egg yolks, scraped vanilla pod and icing sugar; the mixture was spooned into little pleated paper cups and left to dry. (In Germany we used best unsalted butter but when, later, we came to London as hard-up refugees we had to use salted butter and vanilla essence, and when I was married I descended to margarine; I shuddered to think what my daughters would use.)

In those days almonds could only be bought whole with their skins on and so we children used to help with skinning them, which involved immersing them in boiling water and slipping them out of their skins. Sometimes they chose to shoot across the kitchen floor. Some of the peeled almonds were salted for Tante Lotte, my father's sister, because she was a diabetic and unable to eat sweet things. The almonds were tossed in hot oil until they were golden brown, then tipped into a plate full of salt and vigorously stirred.

Every summer the family decamped for a long holiday of two months or so to a farmhouse in the Dolomites, the mountain range in the north of Italy on the border with Austria, during which various members of the family and friends came and went. The journey was by train from Berlin to Munich where we stayed the night in the station hotel. Before bedtime we looked in on the *Bierkeller*, a huge barn of a place set with tables and chairs full of beer-swillers in a smoky and steamy atmosphere with waitresses carrying full tankards of beer on each finger and others bearing loaded trays on their shoulders. As they weaved in and out of the tables, never spilling a drop, they looked as though they were doing a strange dance. We did not stay long because my parents were not interested in alcohol and so we all went to bed. It was very noisy because we could hear the trains shunting in the goods yard outside. Daddy remembered a previous visit, before I was around, when Tommy slept between his parents in a big saggy bed which meant that he slept in the hollow. When a friend asked him where he had slept at the hotel, he answered, 'In the hole'.

Next morning we continued our train journey to be met as usual by a jolly fat Italian called Achille Talenti, a well known architect, in his very smart fawn-coloured sports car. Tommy and I sat outside in the dickey seat with the luggage, while the grown-ups had the more comfortable seats inside. This ride was always the highlight of the holiday for us with our hair streaming behind us as we sped in and out of the hairpin bends down and down until we reached Colfosco. The road was so narrow that two cars could not pass, and the only answer to that problem was for the men to get out and lift the smaller one over the other.

Colfosco was a tiny village in a wide green valley with pine trees on the slopes of the steep Dolomite mountains, with a little church whose bell could be heard from a long way away on Sundays and holidays or when there was a wedding or a funeral. There were farmhouses with large overhanging roofs scattered around and sheep grazing high up in the little meadows. We hired the same house each year from the farmer called Herr Köstner. His elderly father, although completely blind, was shepherd of their flock, taking them up the mountain to graze in spring and coming down again in the autumn with them before the winter snow. I suppose his family kept him supplied with food. As he could not see our faces he used to feel them with his rough hands, which told him what we looked like. A village girl came with the house as cook and maid of all work.

The house had a steeply sloping garden with a wooden fence all round it and at the bottom a wooden bench with a mass of stinging nettles underneath. Because it was always so hot we children only wore pants, and often nothing at all. On one occasion I decided to amuse myself by rolling down the whole length of the garden but I

had forgotten about the nettles and rolled right into them. I screamed and screamed and everyone came running to pick me up, cuddle me and dab me with this and that to stop the pain. In the top corner of the garden opposite the house Onkel Wipp, who came with his son Klaus to stay, made a rockery for the plants he found when climbing the Sassonger, a steep pointed mountain nearby, and he and Mummy planted them there.

Tommy and Klaus, who was his best friend, wore *lederhosen* and boots when they herded the farmer's two goats for him. Sometimes they played their recorders, often with no clothes on at all. I tried to play mine, but no sound came out of it and so I just pretended to play. Mummy played a guitar with coloured ribbons on it and sang Viennese songs, which were mostly slightly vulgar, while we had a rest around the unlit tiled stove. We often joined in with the choruses, such as,

O how useful is the cowpat,
Useful for everything:
In winter for a stomach-warmer,
In summer for a ha–ha–hat;
In winter for a stomach-warmer,
In summer for a hat.

There was another about gypsies which began, 'The gypsies are happy, the gypsies have fun...' but I do not remember the rest. But when a gypsy and her little girl came begging to the door I was filled with fear because I had been warned never to let gypsies take me away, and so I clung to Mummy's skirt and quivered until they had gone. I am still frightened of gypsies.

On a table by the front door there was a pile of straw hats and as you went out you put the top one on your head, and as you came in you put it back on top of the pile. On the kitchen window-sill the cook always put the squeezed-out halves of lemons to dry so that she could use the zest for her cooking, but I used to help myself to them before that, to suck the last drop of juice out of them. I liked sour things and Tommy liked sweet things.

Klaus and I were sitting one day on a rug in the garden where he taught me to tell the time with the aid of his watch, which had a Mickey Mouse decoration on its face, a recent innovation then, but it seemed to do the trick very effectively. On some days the grass was covered with white washing on which the boys were encouraged to pee, thus, with the help of the sun, bleaching the linen to a snowy white with no further need of chemicals. It was, no doubt, washed afterwards.

In the evenings, after supper, everybody made a small pilgrimage along the path by the house to a point from which we had a fine view of the mountains, especially Marmolata, glowing pink in the sunset. I used to sit on a particular stone slab, which was part of the rocky path, pretending it was a car which I drove, while the others were mountain-watching. We often went on walking expeditions in the valley or up the lower slopes wearing our boots and sun hats and carrying little baskets and our walking-sticks. At each new village on the way we bought a little silver disk bearing the name of the village, which

was tacked on to our walking stick by the shopkeeper. We tried to collect as many as possible. The sticks were used to steady walkers on rocky climbs, but also to tap the ground in front of us and frighten away any lurking snakes. We picked wild strawberries and raspberries while banging away, but I never saw a snake though I was terrified even at the thought of meeting one.

Mummy and I went to the village through a field full of ripe corn, very tall and well above my head, with blue cornflowers, white daisies and red poppies growing there as well. Mummy went in front of me and because of her longer strides the corn closed in behind her and she vanished from my sight. I screamed with fear as I could neither see her nor know where I was going. Of course she came back to fetch me, but the only consolation I received was to be told not to be so silly. Although we did not know it, that was to be our last holiday in Colfosco.

Once back in Berlin, we resumed our normal life. Tante Inge, a friend of my father, took me to the children's section of the zoo where I had a ride on a huge woolly sheep, which was so fat that my legs stuck out on either side of it. It was a very cosy seat, but before I dismounted, to my great indignation, Tante Inge inspected my ears to see if they were clean. Mummy would not believe me when I told her about it later. On another occasion she and Daddy went for a walk and I wanted to go with them; the only way they could get rid of me was to take me to a cake shop where I was allowed to choose a pink meringue, and I skipped home with my trophy.

For Christmas that year I was given a sledge, but all the snow had turned to slush. I was determined to try out my new present and bullied Mummy into taking me for a ride in it. It made a fearful screeching sound but I was happy, hardly noticing that my nice clean hand-knitted pale blue angora outfit had become so dreadfully bespattered with mud that it had to be washed. The worst part of removing leggings was pulling the in-step elastic off over my shoes because it was icy cold and wet and my fingers were freezing. I wore the same suit when we went skating. Tennis courts were flooded in the winter so that city people could skate where there were no rivers or lakes. Like everybody else I wore boots with skates attached, but every time I tried to move I fell over and twisted my ankles. I was left crying with cold, clinging to the tennis court wire fence. Onkel Wipp's

second wife had a terrier on a lead who ran on the ice and pulled her along all round the rink: it looked so easy.

Onkel Wipp had an ancient widowed mother called Mamsi (to rhyme with 'clumsy'), a formidable lady who made herself look tragic by wearing pale mauve face powder and a large black hat with a nest of black veiling over it draped down over her face. I spent a lot of time staring at her when she came to tea.

One sunny day Mummy, Tommy, Klaus and I were driven by his father to Grunewald, a large area of trees, walks and open spaces on the edge of Berlin where we could run about freely. We rushed about playing hide-and-seek and looking for interesting-shaped twigs and fir cones when we suddenly came upon a pretty, sunny glade where to our great joy and astonishment we found sweets and chocolates hanging from branches of the trees.

Once a month a sewing lady came to the house to do alterations, mend household linen and make new dresses for us that my mother had designed and cut out. She sat at our treadle machine and sewed all day long, stopping only when it was necessary for me to try on a garment. I hated that, particularly because there were pins involved which sometimes missed their mark.

When Mummy needed to go shopping at the haberdashers, where she bought all the needles, threads, sequins and beads for her fancy dress business, I loved going with her. The road was called Kurfürstendam, the Oxford Street of Berlin. One shop, however, which we needed to pass on the way had outside it a full-size suit of armour complete with vizor. I was totally convinced that it would move and attack me, no matter how much Mummy explained that it was quite empty inside, saying, 'Look, *Mausekönig* (my little mouse-king), I will lift the vizor so that you can see inside.' She lifted me up; I saw and understood, yet the fear never left me and I used to drag her to the other side of the busy road to make a detour. At the far end of the same street was an elegant

sweet-shop in whose window stood a large golliwog holding a box of chocolates with SAROTTI written on it. It had huge black eyes, which rolled from side to side to show how delicious the contents were. I never tired of seeing it and had to be pulled away.

There was also a ladies' dress-shop with a different kind of window display but no less enthralling. A tiny elegant lady dressed in the latest fashion would appear in the far distance slowly coming nearer and nearer and becoming larger and larger until she came up to the window life-size. After her came other models in the same way, and they sauntered back equally gracefully, returning to their tiny size. No wonder I wanted to be a dress-designer when I grew up. I spent most of my time drawing, acquiring quite a reputation, and Mummy showed me how to draw really life-like faces side-view, which thrilled me and kept me busy for ages.

When the parents were going out for the evening they always came to say 'Goodnight' first and I remember the feel of my mother's golden-brown fur coat with its fur buttons and the unforgettable smell of her perfume.

CHAPTER TWO

Exodus

At the age of seven, German children leave their kindergarten to start school. Mine was a short way from home and I was looking forward to going there. My teacher was an old lady, about thirty-five, who had a large bosom which wobbled inside a shiny white blouse. I still dislike that fabric. We sat two to a desk, but memory does not help about our activities except that we were all looking forward to the end of the day. Sure enough there were all the mothers waiting for us, each with a large colourful *Tüte* full of presents, pencils, rubbers, rulers, notebooks, crayons, a pencil-sharpener, and of course some sweets. We skipped home happily clasping our trophies.

When it was someone's birthday the teacher would say 'Whose birthday is it today?' Someone would put their hand up and she would say, 'Come to the front of the class' and would give the child a little card with Mary and her baby Jesus on it or a picture of a saint with a halo. On the seventeenth of October she said the same thing again and to everyone's surprise two girls got up and went to the front of the class. Putti Hübenthal was the first, a teacher's pet because her father was a member of the school staff and a Nazi, and she was given a big hug with a little picture. I, however, the second girl, received nothing. 'You don't get a picture: you're Jewish', she said. I was very upset because she was so unfair and unkind. Until then I had not realised what it meant to be Jewish, but I was finding out.

A little later we heard at school that a bad man was about who stole little children, taking them into a forest to kill them, and we were told to be very careful on our way to and from school and not go along with anyone we did not know. Soon after this, on my way home from school, I saw a dishevelled old man with a beard coming towards me, shuffling along in brown checked slippers, and as soon as he had passed me he turned round and followed me. I was convinced that this was *the* bad man and started to run home as fast as my wobbly legs would take me. Somehow the steps up to the front door were higher and more numerous than usual and the door heavier to open, but I managed it, banged it shut behind me and ran screaming up the four flights of stairs to our flat where Mummy was already at the door wondering what on earth was the matter. I could not tell her, but cried uncontrollably, and after that I had nightmares about the old man in his checked *Pantoffel* slippers.

Another time on my way home from school I stopped to look at a funeral director's window and was enchanted by a very small white coffin with frills of lace all round it. When I got home I told Mummy what I had seen and added, 'It must have been made for the baby of a bride.'

In 1934 Tommy had to go to a new Jewish school because Jews were now segregated, and when they came out of school one day they were attacked by a gang of Nazi youths and poor Tommy came home with a bloody nose. He received the same treatment when he went camping with his schoolmates. The Nazi youths were dressed in a uniform of khaki shirts and shorts with swastika arm-bands.

Many soldiers also were to be seen in the streets, the ones in black uniforms being called S.S. men, also wearing arm-bands with swastikas. A new order was published that all citizens were to put their lights out on a particular evening, and we watched from our window as the S.S. men strutted by in their goose-step march, carrying huge flags and flaming torches singing warlike songs,

> *Die Fahne hoch, die Reihen fest geschlossen...*
> Lift high the flag and tightly close the ranks...

Hitler commanded that once a week everyone had to cook an *Eintopfmahl,* a whole dinner cooked complete over a single gas ring, in order to teach the people to save resources in case of war. This meant boiling the meat in water in the bottom of the saucepan with the vegetables above and the potatoes on top, with the liquid serving as soup. An S.S. man came to each house to inspect the kitchen and see that the order had been carried out When Lina answered the door-bell and saw who was there she said, 'Go away: we're Jewish here', and shut the door in his face. This was a brave thing to do, particularly because she was a Roman Catholic.

The family, along with other Jewish families, took lessons in Hebrew in case they had to emigrate to Israel. We all sat at desks as if we were at school and learned how to write the strange letters starting from the back of the book and the right edge of the page towards the left. This was all very puzzling to me and I was not sure what it was all for.

Hebrew	Sound	Hebrew	Sound	Hebrew	Sound
א	-	ט	T	ע	-
ב	B	י	Y	פ	P/F
ג	G	כ	K	צ	Tz
ד	D	ל	L	ק	K
ה	H	מ	M	ר	R
ו	V	נ	N	ש	S
ז	Z	ס	S	ת	T
ח	Ch				

Life was becoming increasingly difficult for Jews. No Jew could afford to employ an architect any more, and non-Jews were not allowed to employ a Jewish one. It was so in all the professions. Daddy's twin brother, Homi, (his proper name was Helmuth) had gone to England some years previously to work as a picture-restorer at the National Gallery, and he wrote urgently to tell Daddy to come immediately to England even if this meant leaving everything behind, because it was clear that Hitler was intent on getting rid of all Jews. Daddy agreed and left in a great hurry. We could not go with him until he had found a job in England, and so we packed our suitcases and set off for Prague, the capital of Czechoslovakia, to stay with Onkel Wipp. This was Tommy's nick-name for Fritz Cassirer, a newspaper editor who had to leave Berlin just before us because he was anti-Nazi. He had to start all over again in Prague, but after Hitler's invasion of that country, just before the beginning of the Second World War, he migrated to the United States where he stayed for the rest of his life. While we were sitting in the train at Berlin waiting to leave I looked out of the window and to my surprise saw Marion of the birthday cake at the window of another train at the next platform. We called to each other, 'Where are you going?', and I shouted, 'To England', and she answered, 'To Israel'. The train moved off and we never saw each other again.

During our time in Prague, about six months, I went to a school of which I have no recollection, apart from a boy of my age in the class with whom I fell in love. He had black hair and blue eyes and, best of all, a scar just under his left eye, and I used to walk home with him.

My mother made clothes for both of us and her green tweed dress needed a matching leather belt which she had designed and ordered. This entailed a walk to a specialist shop across the River Moldau, and on the way we had to pass some very small cottages built at the side of the river way down below them. This is where the alchemists once lived who were required by the king to make gold for him in their furnaces and glass vessels. They had a time limit and if they had not succeeded by then they were tossed into the river below, where they perished. The belt shop smelt deliciously of leather and Mummy was pleased because the belt had turned out exactly according to her design with fringed ends matching the colours of her dress.

On the way home we stopped in front of Saint Stephen's Church, which had a tower with an unusual clock face. When the clock struck the hour a little door opened at the side and wooden figures of the twelve apostles jerked along on a revolving platform to the opposite door. I could have watched all day.

Tommy and I were thrilled with a self-service food-hall in Wenceslas Square. At the back was a long soup-counter manned by chefs with huge ladles. There were twenty or so varieties to choose from but Tommy always used to choose the garlic because at home garlic and onions were not allowed inside the house. The rolls section intrigued me most. There were towers of open rolls revolving slowly, each sort in a separate glass container with a slot so that when you had paid your money you could extract the roll of your choice. Each roll was made up of several layers of delicacies, and men used to bet on who could eat one without spilling the contents.

On one of our shopping expeditions for vegetables I waited outside the greengrocer's and watched the people go by. Suddenly I noticed a man surreptitiously helping himself to a ring of dried figs from the stall in front of the shop. Thinking that no one was looking he stuffed them inside his coat, and I rushed inside to tell Mummy, but she would not believe me. I thought I would make a good detective.

While we were in Prague I begged to have swimming lessons. Mummy learned by being thrown into the deep end of a pool by her father, but I was treated more humanely with lessons by an instructor who spoke German. He put me on a bench and showed me the necessary movements, then he attached me to a long line hooked to a belt round my waist, and lowered me into the water to start swimming. A well-meaning girl swam up to me and asked the teacher, 'Shall I unfasten her now?', at which point I screamed with fear, sure that I would sink if she did this. End of swimming lessons.

For a special treat Onkel Wipp took me with him on a long train-journey to hunt for the semi-precious stones which he collected. He had several show-cases full of the most beautiful specimens of all colours, shapes and sizes, lit up to display their sparkle. My favourite was an acid yellow citrine, and I still have a small box with tiny samples of many varieties. Hunting for the stones entailed wading through sticky grey mud, which is what I mainly remember.

Eventually we had to pack our bags again, say good-bye to Onkel Wipp, and move to Vienna. There we stayed with Tante Liesel, Mummy's sister, and Onkel Ernst, a doctor, and Hanni their daughter who was seventeen, ten years older than me. The doctor's consulting room was panelled in dark brown wood, which I found distinctly unhygienic: 'It ought to be white', I said, and I believe he changed it soon after we had gone. We visited Mummy's two brothers, Franz and Stefan and their wives and also her aunt Tante Adele, a rather grand and awe-inspiring lady who wore high-necked dresses and sat very upright. I was told later that she suffered from multiple sclerosis, a wasting disease of the muscles, which was the reason why I never saw her walk. My mother had the same illness years later when we were in England.

I wore a most beautiful peach-pink organdie dress with its own pink petticoat complete with little silk roses at the neck, which I had inherited from the Petscheks, friends of the family in Berlin.

Their nanny had packed them, along with three silk combinations, wrapped in tissue paper in a lovely parcel. These combinations were very pretty, but required total undressing for vital processes.

Vienna had a permanent fair, lit up at night with fairy lights, very jolly and noisy. Its main attraction was the *Risenrad*, a giant slowly-turning wheel, which had little baskets hanging from it in which people sat. But no one could persuade me to have a ride as even garden swings made me feel seasick.

After several weeks we said goodbye to these Austrian relatives and, apart from the doctor's family, we never saw them again. They all perished in the Holocaust: my mother's brothers and their wives were taken to Theresienstadt, a concentration camp, where they died, and the old aunt was pushed down the stairs of her flat by the Nazi storm troopers who had come to collect her, and so she too died. Hanni and her family were rescued by the British Hebrew-Christian Alliance who brought them to London, where the parents were supported for the rest of their lives by this charity.

So we packed our bags yet again, for the last stage of the journey by train to England, via Switzerland and France, but strangely enough I remember nothing of that long trek, except that when we had crossed the German frontier, I saw my mother's face relaxing. She had been hiding some paper money in the heel of her shoe. Had she been found out, we would never have reached England.

Changing trains was always an anxious time for me, and to make matters worse, after one of these occasions, I realised that I had left my toy dog Tref behind in the last train. There was no going back, but instead a lot of tears.

CHAPTER THREE

Sanctuary

At last, in the summer of 1935, when I was seven, the family was once more reunited. We arrived in London with the same suitcases we had packed in Berlin 'for a holiday in Prague', as the visa described it, everything else having been left behind. Daddy took us to the studio near Victoria Station belonging to my uncle and aunt, Martin and Lotte Bloch, (she was Daddy's sister) and their daughter, Barbara, with whom I used to play in Berlin. The family was away in Malcesine, on the shore of the Lago di Garda in Italy where Martin ran an annual summer school of painting, and he had allowed us the use of his studio during his absence.

It consisted of one huge room with a wooden floor and slanting windows down one side facing east, because that is the best light for artists to paint by. Several screens hid a gas stove and sink for kitchen, a double bed for bedroom, and a bath and wash basin for bathroom: the lavatory was down a dark corridor outside. I wonder now how our life there was organised. Daddy was out at work most of the time as an assistant architect to a Mr Dugdale, Mummy fed us, though she had never cooked or cleaned before, and I had to do the shopping at the corner shop without a word of English but with the help of a list and a few words learned by heart. Fortunately both parents spoke adequate English, though with a German accent which later embarrassed

Tommy and me, for Daddy had had an English governess when young. We were fortunate in having Mr Dugdale as a guarantor for our family to ensure that we were not a drain on the economy and to support us in the event of our running short of money.

By the time the Blochs returned home Daddy had found a permanent home for us in a flat in Belsizia, in north-west London, where several roads clustered whose names all contained the name 'Belsize' - Belsize Lane, Belsize Park Gardens, Belsize Road, Belsize Avenue and Belsize Square where we lived in a flat at No. 46. In this square, opposite the house, was a church called St Peter's where, many years later, I was married. Once again we were ensconced on the top floor up three flights of steep stairs because Daddy preferred not to hear people walking about above him. In the basement lived Douglas Slocombe, a pianist, whom we heard practising diligently, particularly Liszt's Rhapsody in C Sharp Minor, and when he stumbled he repeated the passage again and again and again until he mastered it. On the ground floor lived Miss Carpenter, the sister of Canon Carpenter (but I did not know what a Canon was) and her lady companion. Miss Carpenter had a club foot which intrigued me greatly as she wore a special shoe which was rather unsightly. After they left, the flat was taken over by a group of Australian ballet dancers including John Cranko who became a famous choreographer. I did my utmost to make friends with them but they were all older than I and were completely wrapped up in their work. I secretly hoped that they would invite me to watch a rehearsal. On the first floor lived a pleasant couple with a young boy about my age who was a genius on the treadle sewing-machine which was kept on the communal landing. He cut out and made up all sorts of clothes that he designed.

Tommy had the unpleasant job of carrying down the waste bucket to the passage outside and emptying it into the dustbin, and he always tried to get out of doing this. He went to school but did not do well. He and Daddy did not get on, resulting in frequent rows. He and I fought ceaselessly until I ended up crying and telling the parents, leading to his being punished, which led to my crying again because I had not wanted this. Oh dear! When we

were in Colfosco I had been able to defend myself by chasing him with earthworms, but here on the third floor there were none.

I also started school, the Regent's Park Open Air School, because my cousins Frank and Robin, the sons of my Uncle Homi and Aunt Anchi, went there, and so I had favourable terms. I used to cycle to their house in St John's Wood on my black third-hand fairy cycle and then the three of us cycled to Regent's Park in the care of Anna, their beloved Czech nanny, who walked alongside. She came with them from Germany and never learned to speak English properly, always producing Anglo-German sentences with a Czech accent. All lessons were taken out of doors unless it rained or snowed, and only then did we fold everything up and retire indoors. We sat on folding chairs at folding tables wearing coats, hats and mittens in winter with a rug clipped round us to keep our legs and feet warm, and I do not remember ever feeling cold. This accorded with the latest educational theories about health and fresh air. I loved the school because we did lots of handwork

and painting, and I learned English without noticing it though I did have to have writing lessons with the tiny children because the German Gothic handwriting which I had learned was so very different from the English script. For those lessons I remember having to squeeze into tiny chairs at tiny desks.

We learned to make woven baskets and later on did real carpentry with the proper adult tools. The first product was a strong stool painted red for my mother in the kitchen on which she kept all the pots and pans for years; it was still in use when I came to clear the flat after her death. The next item was a cabinet with brackets for glass shelves, to be added later, intended for my glass animal collection. When, however, I took it home at the end of my last term, the war started almost at once and it was put into the attic for the duration, shelfless.

Among the children in my class was a pair of identical twins, Janet and Anne, daughters of Anna Zinkeisen, the artist, who brought them to school accompanied by a black miniature poodle whose black fluffy hair exactly matched that of the twins. When we had art lessons we took it in turn to sit still for ten minutes for the rest of the class to paint us, but when it was Janet's turn she and her twin sat in identical poses for twenty minutes altogether, making the end results of our efforts much more satisfactory.

Another classmate, Philip, invited me to his birthday party to which Daddy took me by bus. The house was one of a grand terrace on the edge of Regent's Park and the party was a great success. At the end of it all the nannies came to collect their charges until I was the only one remaining uncollected as Daddy was late as usual. Philip's nanny sent him off to get ready for bed and eventually Daddy arrived to find me ashamed and upset. Philip came down to say good-bye, saying, 'Where's your car?', and Daddy answered, 'Round the corner: it's a red double-decker.'

At the end of each autumn term the husband of the headmistress would give us a thrilling show with string-puppets made by himself. There was an opera-singer and a marvellous pianist who flipped his coat-tails aside before sitting down and twiddling the knobs of his music-stool. He then rolled his cuffs back and began to play vigorously. The performance culminated with a Scottish bagpiper marching back and forth with kilt swinging. This was all accompanied by music on a piano.

After school I often went to Frank and Robin's house in Norfolk Road in the hope that Anchi, their mother, whom I adored, would ask me to stay the night. I had to ring up home to ask permission and it was always granted. Anna, their nanny, slept in the same room as the boys, as I did. Her bed had drawers underneath and when the boys had been tucked up, kissed good-night by all the grown-ups, with the door left open and the landing light on, they would get out of bed, open the drawer where Anna kept her powder box and puff. Each boy put a dollop of powder on his nose and having stowed everything away neatly leapt back into bed. Each put his thumb in his mouth and used his first finger of the same hand to massage the powder into his nose with a circular movement.

Frank and Robin had a large Old English sheepdog called Pucky as well as a tortoise. Pucky, being jolly and bouncy, enjoyed chasing balls and fetching sticks and even tried to make the tortoise run after him but without success. Frank had a friend, Elizabeth, who came to play with us in the garden one day, where someone had left a large empty laundry basket. They persuaded me to climb inside and before I knew what was happening they snapped the lid shut and fastened the catch. I screamed for help until Anchi came to the rescue. No wonder I suffered from claustrophobia ever after.

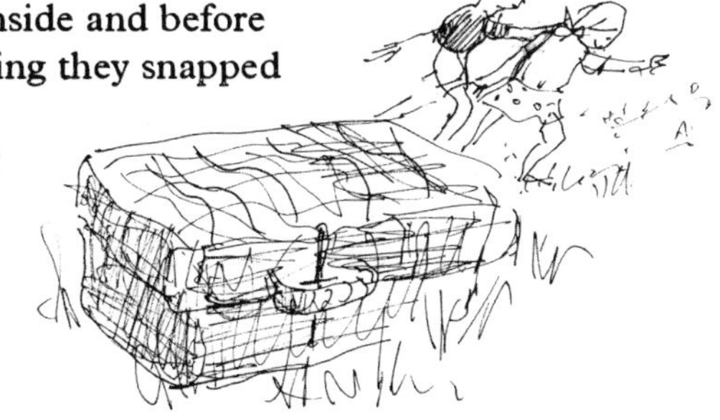

Our flat at No. 46 was reached by a steep flight of stairs from the landing with the sewing machine, where the wallpaper had a very dark pattern which Mummy called *Wanzenschutztapete*, meaning a wallpaper which did not show up creepy-crawlies, though fortunately we did not have any. There were five doors leading off the landing which had an anthracite stove heating the whole flat so that the doors were always open. No central heating for us in those days. Daddy looked after the stove, banking it up skilfully at night so that it stayed in until the morning when he would rattle the grate hard to shake the ash into the pan below. When that had settled and cooled he would tip it into a bucket and either he or Tommy had to take it all the way down to the dustbin. The amount of dust in the hall from this process was unbelievable, and it also spread to all the other rooms, so much so that one could draw pictures in it anywhere in the flat.

Mummy was not a keen housewife but when she started being ill later on we were able to have a charlady once a week. Each week, before she arrived, Mummy would clean the flat herself because she was so ashamed of its appearance. Since Daddy spent much time on the phone in the hall, he discovered that his crêpe-soled shoes were excellent for rolling dust, threads and other grime into neat sausages which he picked up and dropped into the stove so that this area at least was always clean.

Daddy had a knack of dropping in on other people's phone conversations by accident. On one such occasion, hearing two lovers having a dreadful row, he realised that each was too proud to give in to the other and intervened by saying, 'Come on, you two, you know you really love each other; make it up and stop this silly quarrel.' They answered in amazement, 'But who are you?', and he replied, 'I am the Archangel Gabriel', and hung up. On another occasion he answered the phone and the call turned out to be a wrong number. The lady at the other end apologised profusely for the mistake and added, 'I was phoning a friend to invite him to my party, but you sound so much nicer, so why don't *you* come?' He was ever ready to meet new people and so he accepted, had a good time and added the lady to the list of our many friends.

The drawing room had a fireplace with a mantelpiece carrying two candelabra, rescued from Germany and rarely polished, and an armchair on each side for the parents with a rug in each for covering their legs against winter draughts. Opposite the fireplace was a pale pink sofa, which could be transformed into a comfortable bed for Tommy since I had the little room next door. We had a sweet little white kitten that had one blue eye and one green. One day Tommy got up, had breakfast and made his bed before we went off to school and when we came home we could not find the cat anywhere, although there was a faint but distinct sound of mewing from the drawing room. Again we searched and finally Tommy opened up the sofa and out sprang the cat, quite terrified. It rushed to the open window and leapt out. We were three floors up and so Tommy rushed downstairs to rescue it, but it was nowhere to be seen and we never found it.

Our bathroom was long and thin and was used by Mummy for doing the washing in the bath. All the wet clothes would be festooned round the bathroom on lines, clothes-horses and round the stove in the hall. The iron, which she used on the kitchen table, was dangerously plugged in to the twin light-socket dangling overhead. The flex was frayed and the second-hand iron was positively medieval. As she used it, the light swung back and forth casting ominous shadows on the walls.

We never had a washing-machine or a dishwasher or a refrigerator and, as it was difficult to keep food fresh, Daddy made us a larder out of the long window box turned on its side with its back outside and its front towards the kitchen in which we kept all

perishable foods, but for extra freshness milk and butter were kept in wet terracotta containers. When it was very hot the milk did sometimes go sour, and then it was tipped into a muslin square, tied up and hung over a basin to make cream cheese. We had to make endless shopping expeditions, the chief ones being either to Kilburn, which was the cheapest, or to Camden Town. I hated these run-down areas and having to help carry the heavy bags home. Daddy made a shopping trolley from second-hand wheels, a walking stick, and a large cane basket, which embarrassed me greatly. I pretended not to belong to Mummy when she was pulling it. I did, however, enjoy holding her hand as we walked and squeezing it to signal something interesting. She would squeeze mine back on noting it.

The parents' bedroom, like most rooms in the flat, served more than one purpose. Each parent had a couch as far apart as possible so that Daddy would not be disturbed by Mummy's snoring. During his afternoon nap, because he slept lightly, he plugged his ears, covered his face with a white linen towel, and smothered the telephone with cushions. The rest of the household had to tiptoe about. His bedside table was crowded with medicaments and manicure instruments, the latter being used every morning, mainly on his feet. At right angles to the window he had a huge desk with a sloping top like the one in Berlin, with all the paraphernalia of an architect on and around it.

This room was also used as an extension to the drawing room for parties of which there were many. Coffee and home-made continental delicacies were served, but hardly ever any alcohol as this was not my parents' habit. In fact when offered sherry at cocktail parties my father usually refused, but when pressed agreed but added, 'Could you let me have some sugar and a spoon to stir it?'

At Christmas Anchi usually invited the whole Ruhemann tribe with spouses, cousins, uncles and aunts to a huge party in their ample house. There was no sitting down to dinner, but instead huge platefuls of exotic sandwiches, rolls, cakes, strudels and iced honey-cakes were handed round with mulled wine and coffee. The children had an innocent fruit punch. The Christmas tree was wonderfully displayed as the focal point, with tiny, carefully chosen presents hung from the branches, one for each guest. The candles were real and lit, and one twig of the fir tree was burned in the open fire to scent the room – unforgettably.

On New Year's Eve we usually had friends and family to a party whose highlight was, in German, *Blei giessen*, namely lead-pouring. Over the year we had been collecting bits of scrap lead, which were placed into a huge ladle for a fortune-telling session. The ladle was held over a gas flame on the kitchen stove to melt the lead and when it was molten it was poured from a height into a bucket of cold water, whereupon it congealed with much hissing and spluttering into lumps of all sorts of shapes and sizes. When everyone had taken a piece all the lights bar one, a bright table-lamp, were turned off and one by one each person held their lump in front of the light to cast a huge shadow on the opposite wall. The spectators then suggested what the shape foretold, but the owner had the final interpretation.

When I was about ten, around 1937, the Homi family took me with them on a holiday to Brittany, to a village called Le Puldu, near Quimpère, and my pride and joy was a yellow and white striped bathing costume with round yellow buttons down the front which my parents had bought for me. We stayed in a hotel, spending much of the time on a huge empty sandy beach where Homi taught us to float in the lukewarm sea. In the morning we children would potter about sucking delicious toffee lollipops and also gazing with wonder at a lady guest paddling in the sea with several toes missing. The whole family explored the country around, in the course of which we visited a restaurant famous for its *crêpes suzettes* where we watched the cooks pouring ladles of batter into sizzling frying pans, and then when the pancakes were done on one side throwing them up, flipping them over and catching them again in the pan to complete the cooking. After this, orange juice with some liqueur was poured over the pancakes and set alight, to the sound of delighted 'oohs' and 'aahs' from the customers.

Anchi bought me a wooden model of a local fishing boat with a brown sail, though sadly it sank on its first trip. I rescued it and it occupied a proud position on my mantlepiece at home for years. She also gave me two dolls, a boy and a girl, dressed in traditional Quimpère costume, which I still cherish.

My parents could never afford a holiday, but once they sent Tommy and me by ourselves to a farm in Shropshire which we enjoyed enormously and where we never once fought. We helped with hay-making and collecting eggs and other useful jobs, and diverted ourselves with croquet. I spent much of my time drawing, and discovered the perspective of lawn-edges going round corners, progressing to the design of a cake minus its first slice.

In order to make a little extra money my mother painted rubber bathing caps with pretty flowers, shells or fishes for a dealer, and sometimes I would do some of the painting as well. She made clothes for both of us and even her own hats, a skill which she learned in Vienna at art school and later practised professionally at the Wiener Werkstätte, a craft centre founded on *art nouveau* fashions. I was terribly embarrassed when she came to collect me from school wearing one of her creations.

On rare occasions the whole family went to the Odeon cinema at Swiss Cottage where the performance started with Sandy

Macpherson on the theatre organ rising slowly out of the basement illuminated by rainbow colours. He would play several pieces of popular music, then the process was reversed to the accompaniment of the clapping and whistling of an appreciative audience. A short news film would follow, and finally the main feature film. On the way home Tommy and the parents chatted critically about the film, but I was grumpy and hung back because I wanted to savour the memory of the film. Sometimes Tommy and I would go to the same cinema on a Saturday morning by ourselves, joining the long queue of children to see such stars as Charlie Chaplin, the Marx Brothers, Shirley Temple and Deanna Durbin. Some films were so thrilling or frightening as to give me nightmares which made me run for comfort to the parents, but I had to brave the shadows cast by the all-night-burning stove which were nearly as frightening as the dreams, and also the wrath of my father if he was woken up.

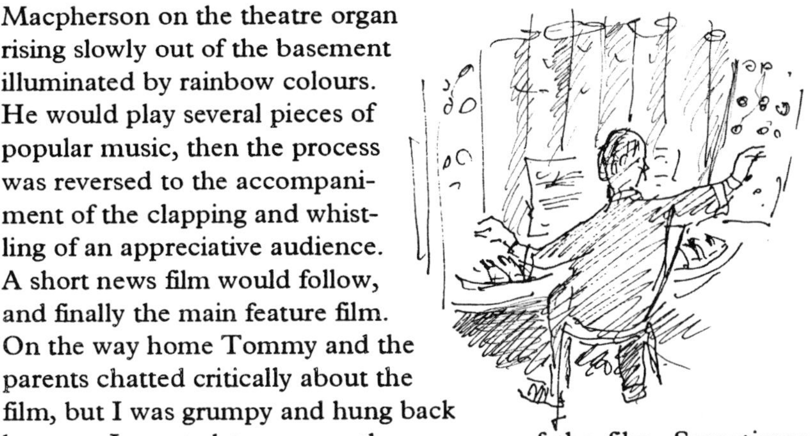

I was once invited to the pictures by a schoolboy, the son of friends of my parents, who wore a pink blazer with grey stripes, a pink cap and grey shorts, but I did not know how to respond to the invitation being quite unclear about the financial arrangements, and declined the offer, later regretting it. His name was Paul Hamburger (later Paul Hamlin, the publisher). He was very fond of money even as a small boy. His uncle once made a rash offer to give him anything he wanted for his birthday and he immediately answered, 'I would like some shares in Woolworths.'

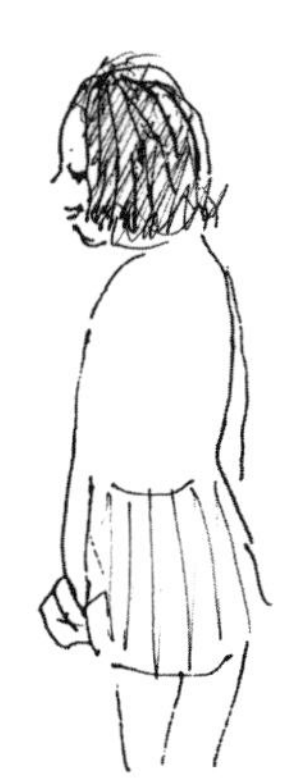

About 1938, to my great joy, Miriam Landsberger, my dear friend from Berlin, arrived with her brother Peter to live with their aunt in London not far from us. Her parents had sent them over from Germany for safety but they stayed on: he was Jewish but his wife was Roman Catholic and so they were not obliged to leave, but we heard later that he had been compelled to work in a wire cable factory and was forbidden to travel during the rush-hour so that the day was long, the work hard, and he received little if any pay. Towards the end of the war his wife committed suicide and he died from 'natural causes'.

Miriam and I resumed our friendship, and as she did not get on with her aunt she spent much time in our house. We played at shop window-dressing with a hairdresser's plaster model head which I had been given for my birthday, at my request. To my great disappointment it only had painted hair and not the luxuriant tresses I had seen in the shop, but we draped filmy scarves around it and plied her with eye make-up and lipstick. We filled empty bottles with liquid to look like nail varnish and made lipstick out of coloured wax. When she was grown up Miriam married a divorced film actor, Herbert Lom. She said to him, 'If you are ever unfaithful to me I will commit suicide.' Later he was, and she did.

Some months after we had settled in Belsize Square a crate arrived for us from Berlin packed by Miriam's father. Unpacking it felt like Christmas, but my parents were disappointed that it contained mainly silver and ornaments rather than useful household items. I, however, was overjoyed when my precious white folding doll's pram emerged and it could again stand by my bedside, even if some of my dolls were not included.

There was, however, a quantity of fine Meissen porcelain china of *Zwiebelmuster* (onion design) that my mother had been given as a wedding present, 'twelve of everything', plates, bowls, soup tureens, gravy boats and the rest, and her sister, Tante Liesel, also had 'twelve of everything'. This combined collection had been given to their mother at her wedding in the eighteen-nineties. Towards the end of the war my mother started a long decline with multiple sclerosis which caused her to knock things over and led to every piece of the service being chipped or broken by the time she died. Years later when Hugh, my husband, and I visited Berlin we called at the Meissen shop in Kurfürstendamm intent on buying a piece of the same design for old time's sake but were dismayed to find that a dinner plate was priced at around fifty pounds. The assistant rather grudgingly mentioned that there were some seconds, and even some thirds, in a back room, and we eventually settled for a six-inch bowl of the last sort.

Often in summer my father would arrive home bearing a huge bundle of flowers and branches of lilac or apple-blossom or whatever was in season so that one could hardly see his face. These he had gathered from empty properties when inspecting them for prospective clients. In Berlin we had a little garden some way from the flat, which was more like an allotment, but here in London we only had a window-box outside the drawing room. As soon as he came home he filled the bath with cold water and immersed his precious burden until he was ready to arrange them – his speciality.

Tommy as a teenager had some strange habits, one of which was standing outside the house, hands in pockets, watching the world go by. One day a policeman came by and told him not to loiter but move on, to which Tommy replied, 'I'm only standing outside my own house'.

In summer we could hear the bell of the Walls ice-cream man on his tricycle and we had to inveigle the parents into the wild extravagance of iced lollies for us, and even tubs for themselves. As the lid was lifted from the large box on the front, clouds of steam rose up from the carbon dioxide that kept the contents cold. The coalman came with a horse and cart looking very grimy, with a leather head-piece which continued right down his back. He stood with his back to the cart and hoisted the sack on to his back with his hands over his shoulders, and carried it down the side of our house past the dustbin to our coal-chute where he managed to tip it down over his head.

As Daddy often ran out of ready money he used to send me with a note for the bank clerk at Swiss Cottage, who gave me the cash without batting an eyelid. I grew quite fond of him, not least because he had a scar under his left eye just like my Czech boyfriend, and when Daddy and I went together to the bank we all had a pleasant chat.

People from all over the world lived in Belsizia, particularly Jewish refugees from Eastern Europe, but sometimes I saw a brown man with a white cloth wound round his lean body and sandals on his bare feet. This was Gandhi, the Indian politician, from whom I gained my nickname at nursery school.

At home the radio was always on, playing classical music, at least when Tommy was there, and he and Mummy used to compete at recognising the composer in the shortest time. My father, on the other hand, was completely tone-deaf and could only recog- recognise one tune, a Strauss waltz, because of its rhythm. In due course I asked for piano lessons and a lady was found to teach me in her flat. She was a German refugee who had married an English composer much younger than herself in order to obtain British citizenship without a wait of the statutory five years. In her endeavours to look as young as her husband she dyed her grey hair black and rubbed all manner of creams into her face and hands while she sat next to me at the piano. The smell was nauseating.

Unfortunately we had no piano at home and I was expected to practise on a length of cardboard with the black and white notes printed on it. Not surprisingly I made little progress and soon the lessons were stopped.

My pocket money amounted for years to a penny a week and my brother had twopence and so it took ages to accumulate enough to buy anything worthwhile, but I set my heart on buying a baby doll which came in a grey cardboard box with a metal clasp. She had a little hole between her painted lips and a corresponding hole further down, and came packed with a feeding bottle, teat and nappies. When she was fed with 'milk', she was able, in due course, to wet her nappies. How I coveted her! I saved and saved for what seemed like years, and eventually I was able to buy her, but by then I had quite lost interest in baby dolls and I was totally disappointed with her. Actually I had suspected long before that this might be so, but my pride would not allow me to back down. My next target was a Baby Brownie camera, square and black, which took excellent black and white photographs, rather small, but it proved to be a wonderful investment, which I used for years.

On bank holidays a fair would arrive on Hampstead Heath to which Tommy and I would go together, armed with a little extra pocket money. We always headed straight for the 'bumpums', little brightly-coloured electric cars surrounded by rubber fenders. A sixpenny ride ended much too soon as we liked to drive round avoiding the collisions which other drivers enjoyed. I did not like roundabouts, except to look at, because they made me feel sick, but the pink candy floss was irresistible even if it had more colour

than taste. I loved the music and the flashing lights but I hated the pushing crowds. The two stalls not to be missed were the hoop-la, giving goldfishes in prizes, and the gypsy who sold tiny penknives which Tommy dismissed as useless rubbish, although they had real blades which cut, but which I wanted to add to my collection of miniatures – glass animals, tiny pipe-cleaner dolls, and tea-sets.

On Sunday mornings Daddy and I had the habit of going for a long walk on the Heath hand in hand when we discussed the ways of the world and sex in particular as my mother was not forthcoming on that subject. Sometimes he walked behind me and once when he caught up he remarked, 'Did you know your left leg is thinner than your right? You ought to give it some extra exercise because you will never get a husband if your legs don't match.' He had fixed ideas of what was suitable for me, and had little time for my various experimental hair styles.

Hampstead Heath was also useful for picnics at weekends, when along with a great number of other families we would find a place with a view under a tree and pretend we were in the country. I had a new kite, which fulfilled a life-long ambition, and I could not wait to give it its first flight. I was deemed to be unable to launch it and so my father and Tommy took it and raced about until it was airborne while I had to chase after them crying, 'Now let me have a go: it's mine and I want to fly it'. They replied, 'Just a minute: we'll get it higher for you first.' At that moment another kite entangled itself with mine and snapped my string. Mine flew free and disappeared out of my sight – for ever. I had never even held it, and was never more deeply upset in my life. My anger and disappointment were only overcome years later when I was able to buy kites for my own children and help them with the launching.

At this time I became anaemic and cod liver oil tablets were prescribed instead of the liquid form which I could not stomach. But I also hated swallowing these Smartie-sized pills and when no one was looking I spat them out into the sink. Since these cost money, which my parents could ill afford, this increased my feelings of guilt, and my sallow complexion remained. Eating meat fat was also an abomination and since it was a rule that nothing should be left on the plate, 'Eat it up, darling, fat is good for you', I kept it in my mouth until the end of the meal and then disposed of it into the lavatory.

Eventually I was eleven, in 1938, time for me to leave the Open Air School and go to Parliament Hill Girls' Grammar School on the other side of Hampstead Heath, in uniform for the first time. This consisted of a navy blue tunic and a white blouse with a red and blue tie that slotted through a loop at the neck and consequently needed no tying. The statutory lisle stockings required a new item for my wardrobe, a pink suspender-belt which made me feel very grown-up and somewhat embarrassed. Winter required a heavy navy belted coat and a velour hat to match with a band of school colours and, of course, elastic under the chin. In summer we had blue-and-white checked dresses with matching knickers, all home-made, with a blazer, second-hand of course, because very little in our house was brand new.

The journey to school meant a twenty-minute walk to Pond Street to catch a train on the North London line to Gospel Oak station and then a few minutes more walk, but a not unpleasant journey because there were always friends on the train. Several of us quickly formed a club called the 'Pegarbs', a title formed from the initial letters of our various Christian names, Peggy, Ellen, a fat girl with black corkscrew curls like Shirley Temple's, Giesela, another German refugee who later won a prize for the best reading of English prose in the school, Annie who was thin, fair and small, Reni, which had always been the short form of my name, Beryl, the ringleader, with ginger hair and freckles, and Susan, whom I cannot remember at all. We also devised a secret language.

Only a few teachers stand out in my memory. The first was the domestic science teacher, Nora Rawbone, but we called her Gnaw A Raw Bone, who taught us sewing, all by hand, the first item being a shoe bag followed by the embroidering of my name on it, all of which took ages, much longer than making it on our treadle machine at home. One afternoon someone fooled about in class and so she made us all stay in after school, a particularly brutal punishment because we could see a long-awaited sale being held in the playground for which a Chinese pupil had made some exquisite baubles of card in unusual shapes and silk threads in beautiful colours complete with tassels. There were only a few, which went to the first buyers, and we missed this unrepeatable opportunity.

Our maths teacher was enormously fat and reposing on her ample bosom was a large collection of brooches and necklaces which earned the description, 'Miss Millington's Flower Garden'. Art lessons were, of course, the best. Our teacher had been a pupil of Marion Richardson, well known for teaching beautiful handwriting to children, which she passed on to us. She encouraged us to paint imaginative pictures, which were displayed around the school. One of mine won first prize in a newspaper art competition.

Tommy was at a nearby school but was not doing well. He did not seem to settle and was eventually seen by an educational psychiatrist who said that he was a brilliant boy but his treatment by the Nazis and his uprooting from Berlin had taken their toll. His main compensation was eating sweet things, which proved to be his undoing in later life when he developed diabetes.

That year must have passed very quickly because in no time at all it was September 1939, and with it came the declaration of war on Germany. This meant the dashing of our hopes for naturalisation in 1940 for which we were yearning, and another total upheaval for all the family.

CHAPTER FOUR

From Pillar to Post

War with Germany began on the second of September 1939, and in no time at all, in expectation of heavy air raids, school children were bundled off to safety out of London. Most of my school went off *en bloc* in one train, each of us kitted out with a small suitcase filled with essential clothing, a gas mask in a square cardboard box hung round the neck, and a label bearing our name and school on our coats. Parents came to see us off, and I am surprised that I do not remember being upset in any way at the parting. It all happened so swiftly that, being used to change, it was just another move, perhaps even an exciting adventure with my friends. It must have been far more of a wrench for the parents.

The trainful of bewildered schoolgirls stopped at London Colney, near Saint Albans, where our teachers guided us to our temporary 'billets', a new word which over the next year would become very familiar to all of us. Giesela and Inge, who were sisters, and I were taken to a council house where we were entrusted to the care of a soldier's wife with a baby, who had been given no prior warning of our arrival. All three of us slept in the marital bed, two parallel and the smallest, Inge, across our feet.

After breakfast we were sent out to play in the street and told not to come in till lunchtime. None of us had ever played in the street before. I was stung by a wasp and had to contravene the 'not till lunch' rule, but I was given a blue bag to clap on to the sting and sent out again. (A blue bag was a small twisted piece of material containing some blue dye that was added to white washing to make it look whiter, a rather different process from that used in Colfosco.) I have no idea how long we had to endure these arrangements including the lukewarm cocoa at bedtime made with water instead of milk, but it was only a temporary stay, thank goodness.

We were then moved to St Albans where we were billeted in the vicarage with a large number of other girls from our school in a dormitory hastily arranged in the attic. The vicar's wife was friendly and motherly and appreciated my help in making a huge jelly for the whole company for pudding. Before it was quite set I had to beat it with a rotary whisk until it foamed and grew to double its size, thus making it go further. For me the jelly was a disappointment, tasting nothing like raspberries but more like cheap pink sweets.

There came another move when more permanent places had been found for us, still in St Albans. This time two of us, Hilda (another Jewish refugee) and I were billeted with Mrs Williamson in Station Road, who asked us to call her Auntie Mabel. She was a retired head-mistress, full of fun, chatter and information. She had a Communist son at the university, which opened up a new field for me, but with her help I began to understand it. Hilda and I had to share a bed, which made me dislike her more than I might have done: I really wanted Auntie Mabel to myself. The long narrow bathroom sported an enamelled bath with lion's claws, and towering above it a terrifying geyser. When the hot tap was turned on, it burst into action with a mighty roar, flashing flames from a little window in the front of its case. I was so frightened of it that I rarely had a bath. It was freezing cold in both the bathroom and the bedroom with no double-glazing or central heating, but in those days that was normal.

Auntie Mabel and Hilda did not get on, which meant that before long we both had to leave this friendly household. I had been very happy there, not least because I was taught how to embroider and make carpets by hooking wool through canvas. All her stair carpets were made like this, but in mauve, pink and purple which were not my favourite colours. Hilda went home for holidays when the air raids permitted and during one of these my foster-mother made me a really grown-up costume of rust-coloured tweed which I adored. (I was only eleven.)

Our school shared buildings with St Alban's High School, their pupils using them every morning and the evacuees every afternoon, each with their own teachers. This meant that by the time we came out in the late afternoon it was usually dark, and wartime precautions forbade street-lighting, with all buildings blacked out so that not a chink of light showed that might have given away positions to enemy bombers. Air raid wardens patrolled to warn you if a light from a window was visible. When we came out of school we were divided into areas of the town and a prefect with a torch led each group to its billets.

The gymnasium of this school was the pride and joy of the headmistress because it was brand new and boasted such a special wooden floor that everyone on entering had to wear asbestos-soled shoes which would not scratch the floor. (No one knew in those days about the danger of close personal contact with this fibre.)

Piano-playing had been a non-starter in London but in St Albans I was offered the chance of having violin lessons which I jumped at, but there was a snag. The way to the teacher's house went past a tramp's shack and I was terrified that he would come out and pounce on me, so that I raced past it as fast as I could, arriving in a sweat with shaking hands and pounding heart. I could hardly concentrate on the lesson because I was already worrying about the return journey. Again the lessons did not continue for long, and again I told no one about my fears. In fact I never caught sight of the tramp.

After leaving Auntie Mabel I was billeted, along with a new companion called Freda, on an eighty-year-old lady and her daughter whom we called Miss Betty. They treated us as if were children of five though I am sure they both meant well. The best thing was that we did not have to share a bed again. Miss B. had a minute silky-haired Yorkshire terrier called Miss Muffet who was allowed in the garden, though we were not. Miss Muffet went for walks with Miss B. on a long lead, which was hauled in on sight of another dog and she was promptly tucked under Miss B.'s arm. Miss B. had a crisp white roll for breakfast but we had sliced white bread (which actually was not white because wartime 'national' bread was pale grey). Worse still, Miss B. ate only the soft middles leaving the crunchy crust on her plate for which I would have given my bottom dollar.

At home I had helped with cooking, baking, dusting and hoovering but none of these was allowed here. Deprived of these activities I became very unhappy and badly behaved for the first time ever. When Miss B. was out of the breakfast room I poured hot tea into the plant pot on the table. I also kept an illustrated diary in which I drew a cruel likeness of her and deliberately left it open on my bedroom table.

There were frequent air-raid warnings with howling sirens when everyone had to seek shelter, some in underground refuges in the garden, others crouching beneath the stairs or under the dining room table. In London people even slept in Underground stations on the platforms. For these occasions Miss B. made grey scratchy

flannel trousers for us to put on over our pyjamas and in these we would rush downstairs to take shelter. Invigorated with hot cocoa, this time made with milk, we waited for the All Clear.

Every morning we were woken by Miss B. carrying a large jug of hot water for washing, but first she would stand at the foot of our beds to say prayers, which we both found embarrassing, and we used to start dressing under the bed-clothes while she had her eyes closed. Eventually Freda left under a cloud on account of some misappropriations. I too left be-cause I was unhappy and also because there was a lull in the air-raids on London, and so I was able to return home and go to what

remained of Parliament Hill School. There were sporadic alarms and in one of these I had to dash into an air-raid shelter on my way home from school in the middle of Hampstead Heath, abandoning my bike at the entrance.

I was not the only member of the family to have been sent away when war broke out. Most of the Jewish male refugees were dispatched to the Isle of Man for their backgrounds to be investigated for fear of spies among their number, and my father and brother and Uncle Martin were detained as 'enemy aliens' until they were cleared. The only way to hasten this lengthy process was to volunteer for the Pioneer Corps, which Tommy did. My uncle, being a painter, took his sketch-book with him and on his return painted several pictures from them, including one of a group of internees at table eating herrings, their staple food, but one of the fishes had turned into a mermaid. He was so happy to be back that he picked a bunch of flowers in the garden, stuck them in a jug and painted them against a bright yellow back-ground, a picture which has pride of place in our drawing room.

Tommy had a brief career as a soldier, being soon invalided out with a crop of boils on his neck. He later found a job in a travel agency and, being good at languages, qualified as an official London guide and could be seen with a black furled umbrella held high leading strings of visitors not only round the city but to many other sights in England and Scotland. His clients thought he was marvellous, giving him generous tips including several boxes of expensive cigars. He received them gladly although he did not smoke. After his death we found piles of cigars in his flat including some very strong and very stale black twisted ones. I gave

these to some homeless men in a day centre where I worked as a volunteer, whose taste buds were not as sensitive as they had been. They smoked them with relish and asked for more.

When the raids started up again Anchi phoned my parents to see if they would let her look after me in Gloucestershire where Homi was looking after some of the pictures from the National Gallery. Others had been dispersed to several manor houses in Gloucestershire, and also to caves in Wales and other sites in Scotland.

Memories of arriving at Anchi's place are vague. Being about twelve I was no doubt put on a train in the care of some kind-looking lady and collected at the other end by the family. At first the Ruhemanns stayed at Solomon's Court Farm and I with neighbours, the Peebles. In the daytime we were all together but I dined and slept in the grandest establishment I had ever encountered. Mrs Peebles lived there with her teenage daughter Joanna and numerous servants including a butler who waited on us

at table, lit the Cona coffee machine for madam after dinner, passed round chocolate mints on a silver salver, and then vanished. (In those days it was quite common for people with large properties to take in evacuees.)

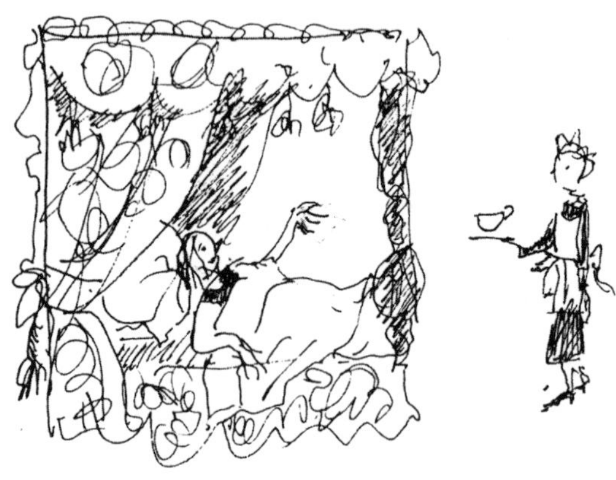

I had a vast bedroom to myself and (what bliss!) a four-poster bed with curtains. Behind what looked like a wardrobe door was a wash basin with places for flannels, toothbrushes towels and such like - the height of elegance. I pretended I was a princess. In the mornings I was woken with a knock on the door by the chamber-maid with early morning tea for 'Miss'. I thanked her in a princess-like manner, motioning her to place it on the bedside table. I really disliked early morning tea, but relished the performance and when she had gone out I poured the tea down my wash basin.

Joanna had an even grander bedroom complete with a walk-in wardrobe, something completely new to me. I had never seen so many clothes in one place before, except in a shop. There were rails full of skirts, dresses and coats, shelves with twin-sets in all the colours of the rainbow and Cheltenham hats to match. She always wore a twin-set with matching skirt complete with pearl necklace. They had a gardener and a gardener's boy with whom I fell in love, but I decided that he fell beneath my dignity as a princess, and so I only waved my white-gloved hand to him from the car in which I was driven by the chauffeur to Solomon's Court Farm each morning.

My cousins and I quickly made friends with Anthony Furse, the ten-year old farmer's son who took us three for a bareback ride on his pony over the hilly farm land with Frank in front, me in the middle and Robin clinging on behind. At one point while going up a steep hill we heard yells and screams from Robin as he slipped down the back of the horse and held on to the horse's tail for dear life. Another escapade had us clambering up a tall ladder into the silage bin where we fooled about on the top layer of vegetation. One by one the boys climbed down again but before I could follow they had taken the ladder away. My screams of rage soon brought help and comfort from the farmer.

Mr Furse kept a flock of sheep which he sheared himself, with the wool being spun and dyed elsewhere. Then he knitted all the family jumpers himself in his spare time. This impressed me greatly because most men in those days would not be seen dead engaged in what was considered to be women's work. Anthony had a loom on which he was weaving a scarf from the same wool and, as I was already madly in love with him, this greatly increased my admiration for him. He gave the finished article to Homi, but when we met again as grown-ups he told me that he had meant it for me but had been too shy to give it to me. We both, it seemed, missed a great opportunity.

We moved again, this time to the Dower House at Avening Court, near Stroud. It had been converted from two cottages which meant that the dining room and drawing room were separated by two doors with a gap between, and here we huddled for safety during the frequent air-raid warnings, since we were

uncomfortably near Aston Down aerodrome. Just by the side of this house was an immense old fir tree, which Robin climbed right to the very tip. He called his mother out to come and look, but she was terrified by the sight and rushed back indoors to hide her fear and trembling while Robin descended safely, but he had to promise never to climb so high again.

Pucki, their old English sheepdog, was adored by all the family and was allowed to go wherever he liked, but occasionally it was clear that a bath was necessary which was anathema to him. Standing in the water he hung his head in misery as he became thinner and thinner with all the soap and water until he looked more like a tailless rat than a dog. In desperation he would attempt an escape, shaking himself and soaking everyone and everything in sight. When he eventually emerged from this performance, clean, dried, and unbelievably beautiful, he lay stretched out by the fire revelling in all the attention. Suddenly he was gone, and despite our hunting high and low, we could find no trace of him and all that remained was to shut the front door and go to bed. Next morning a bedraggled dog presented himself, not only dirty but also smelling horribly of something unmentionable in which he had rolled up to his ears. There was nothing for it but to drag him back into the bath tub and start all over again.

Frank and Robin went to the local school but in the holidays Anchi took us for long cycle rides, one as far as Tetbury, with Robin on his fairy cycle pedalling furiously to keep up. He combined his cycling prowess with skill at aeroplane-spotting, but the sight of a Lysander overhead resulted in an undignified spill into a hedge. The bicycle was the main method of transport because petrol rationing made long car journeys impossible. In fact none of our wider family ever owned a car either before or after the war.

Our next home was the gardener's cottage in the grounds of Sudeley Castle near Winchcombe, lent to Homi for his family, along with half a large greenhouse for a studio in which to attend to the precious paintings stored in the castle. The other half provided tomatoes for the estate, and today the smell of tomatoes always takes me back to that greenhouse. There was not enough room in the cottage for the two boys because of my presence and so they slept in a tent winter and summer in the garden, trotting off with their blankets and hot water bottles each evening.

Frank and Robin played with the owner's son, mostly shooting with airguns on the estate, and occasionally Lady B. would send for 'the girl' to come and play with their daughter Catherine who was about my age. These children lived in a separate wing of the castle from their parents, seeing them only occasionally, being looked after by a nurse and a nursemaid. When I went to tea there in the nursery we were watched over by nanny, though sometimes Lady B. came in from the garden wearing her bee hat and veil with a trug of flowers on her arm and secateurs in her hand. I thought her very grand and I kept rather quiet until she had gone. Catherine showed me round the castle and into a tiny low room in which Catherine Parr, one of Henry VIII's wives, was said to have lived. I remember it as being covered in red velvet, but maybe that was only the showcase containing one of Catherine Parr's teeth among other treasures.

CHAPTER FIVE

Into Another Country

All the pictures having been checked in Gloucestershire we all moved to Bangor in North Wales near the slate mines, where more pictures from the National Gallery were stored. We lived in part of a large house with a landlady who had a lilting up-and-down Welsh voice. When I had made a piece of craft work she would compliment me by saying, 'Isn't she handy? Anchi cooked in the kitchen in the cellar and we helped with the washing up there. Often Robin pretended that the old mangle in the corner was an altar where he dressed up as a clergyman in tea towels and mumbled long services, making us all laugh.

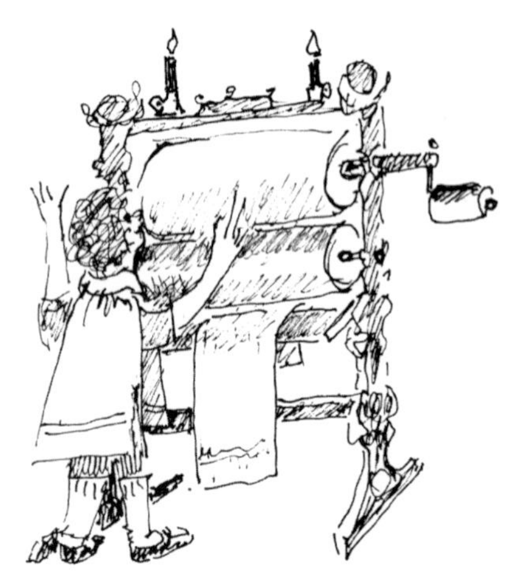

Frank and Robin and I each had a favourite stuffed toy animal about six inches high, mine being the little teddy that I had had on my scooter in Berlin. We played endless games with them, pretending that they were firemen or soldiers or whatever else our imagination conjured up, rushing off in non-

existent cars with brrm...brrm... noises taking their place. After we had gone to bed Anchi spent the winter evenings making outfits for these little toys, and when we woke up in the morning there might be, by our beds, a sou'wester for one, a pair of field-glasses for another, and a coat for the third. Nothing could have pleased us more.

Food rationing resulted in people being encouraged to boost their vitamin intake by venturing into the hedgerows to gather items like rose-hips, blackberries and nettles. The first were collected by schoolchildren with their teachers to be made into rose-hip syrup, rich in vitamin C, for the young; the blackberries were for jam and puddings; nettles were cooked for soup or 'spinach'. Anchi sent us out into the fields with

leather gloves on and a huge basket to pick these stinging nettles, but only the young leaves. When they were cooked they were much reduced in quantity but were delicious. On one of these occasions I had Pucki with me on the lead and failed to notice a herd of cows at the top of the field coming towards us to see what sort of a cow the sheepdog was. I was scared in case they would harm us and fled with Toby to the fence over which we clambered with the cows in hot pursuit.

I went to school at the Bangor County School for Girls wearing a scarlet blazer and grey tunic (second-hand, again). The art teacher, my favourite, was Miss Smart and we exchanged Christmas cards until long after I was married. About a year later Homi and his family moved on, to Glasgow, but they felt that I ought not to change school yet again, and so I became a miserable boarder. One upsetting consequence of this was that I had to abandon my best friend, a day-girl, because of pressure from the

boarders. Mrs Arnold ('Mrs A.') was the strict Matron, an entirely square figure wearing large glasses through or over which she glared at us while we did our homework, in deathly silence. Behind her was an Edwardian over-mantle in dark brown oak ornamented with empty niches, and on the wall above sneered a sepia reproduction of the Mona Lisa. I have disliked that picture ever since, even after seeing the original in the Louvre. There was also a cook who was a fellow-conspirator with Mrs A, whom I particularly disliked because she called me a Nazi. 'Stupid woman', I said to myself, 'Why did she think we had to leave Germany if we were Nazis?' Food being rationed, with cheese in minute portions per week, we wondered why we never had any to eat even though the smell of cheese often assailed our nostrils. I was the leader of a revolution to demand our rights, especially because I liked cheese, and thereafter we had it every week.

There were about thirty boarders of two kinds, either termly, like myself, or weekly. The former only went home for the main holidays, air raids permitting, but the latter could go home for week-ends, but with luck a T.B. might be invited by a W.B. home for a break. This did not always work out happily. Nancy invited me, and once more I had to share a bed, and when her friends came to play all of them spoke Welsh together which was a foreign language to me, and so I was left out of everything. In addition, we had tea before breakfast and with it; tea for elevenses; tea after lunch; tea for tea; tea with supper; and tea at bedtime. I cannot remember what we had to eat, but I was glad to go back to the boarding house.

My best friend was Eileen as she always had good ideas about what games to play and what events to arrange for people's birthdays. We all used to pool our pocket money for this and went shopping to a wonderful stationer's for rubbers, pencils, pencil-sharpeners, foreign stamps, stamp albums, notebooks and pretty wrapping paper. When it was fine we used to play in the hilly garden, full of laurel bushes and trees, but Eileen preferred to sit in the crook of a branch, her head in a book. Many years later she told me that she was not reading but crying her eyes out with home-sickness.

At school we started the day with prayers which were always in Welsh, but I never learned much more than the Lord's Prayer, along with the Welsh National Anthem, and a few rude phrases. The headmistress was another squat and square lady with whom I am pleased to say I had very little to do.

One day some friends of the Ruhemanns, by the name of Dodd, invited me to their home. They had a great many children and lived in jolly chaos, which made a pleasant change. The father taught at the University of Bangor and his brother was a leading theologian at Cambridge where he taught my future husband; his daughter became godmother to our daughter Isobel.

My father's firm, and my father along with them, had recently moved to Wokingham in Berkshire which meant that I could join my parents again and leave the boarding house with a sigh of relief. Travelling from Bangor I had to go via London with several cases and my bicycle. Place-names had been removed from all signposts, including railway stations, as a precaution against invading troops, and at one of our stops, thinking the guard had called out 'London', I hastily gathered up all my belongings including the bike from the guard's van and jumped on to the platform, only to discover that it was Rugby. So I had to rush everything back into the train before it moved off again. I had hated train travel ever since seeing off my mother from Berlin on her visits to her sister, Tante Lisel, in Vienna, particularly because my father insisted on going into the carriage to help her with the luggage and I was terrified that the train would whisk him away.

At first we lived in rooms next door to the railway station where we were kept awake at night by the shunting of goods trains, but soon we were able to move to Crowthorne in the countryside, into a small bungalow with a big garden. My mother answered an advertisement for growing your own mushrooms and, in preparation for this, obtained a load of manure from the local dairy. Despite this care no mushrooms grew, which was attributed to the horses having been fed on the wrong fodder. In the autumn Daddy and I remedied the situation by going to the nearby woods to hunt edible fungi. He knew all the various kinds and taught me how to tell the good from the bad. There was also a plentiful supply of sweet chestnuts in the same wood.

At this time I was about to start at my fifth new school and decided that it was a good opportunity to give up my name 'Reni', a childish diminutive, in favour of my proper name 'Renate'. The journey to school in Bracknell entailed a five-mile cycle ride through wooded crown lands where there was always the fear that soldiers stationed nearby would jump out of the bushes at me. To see other school friends to ride with for company was a great relief. In the rain we put on yellow waxed capes with sou'westers on our heads but

the water always made its way down the back of our necks to our total misery.

The headmaster, known to us as Bimmy, and his staff were pleasant but rather aged, because all the younger ones had been called up either for military service or for work on the land or in factories. At my first gym lesson I was pleasantly surprised to meet again Miss Mostyn, my games teacher at Parliament Hill School. She was one of the younger ones and was Jewish, with black curly hair and beautiful black eyes. She spent a whole term teaching us backhand at tennis, which seemed tedious at the time but had the happy result that my backhand was always more powerful than my forehand.

One day, in a Scripture lesson taken by a clergyman, Jews became the subject under discussion. A boy said, 'Jews smell'; another, 'They cheat', and another, 'They're ugly'. I became hotter and hotter under the collar until in the end I found myself standing up and saying, 'I'm Jewish: do you think I smell more than you? Do I cheat? Am I uglier than you?' They were all stunned and there was an awesome hush. Then the teacher got up and made some apology for them all, but I cannot remember what he said because I was shaking from head to foot from my first defence of Judaism. I had not realised that I had it in me: I had not realised that I cared so much about it - the words just came into my mouth.

After a while, Daddy's firm went back to London, which meant that my parents had to go too. Once more I was going to stay behind so as not to miss more schooling. School Certificate was looming.

CHAPTER SIX

The Perkinses

My father went to the nearest phone box to phone the billeting officer. 'Yes', she said, 'we have two places available. One is with a policeman's family, and the other is with Mrs Perkins. Which would you prefer?' Daddy leant out of the phone box and said, 'It's either the policeman's family or Mrs Perkins. Which would you prefer?' I did not hesitate for one moment. 'Mrs Perkins', I said, and that turned out to be the best decision of my life. Daddy rang Mrs Perkins there and then, who answered, 'Yes, we can have your daughter, but we're going out this evening.' Despite this warning we went straight to her house in Bracknell with my suitcase, and were warmly welcomed by her, her husband, and George the bandy-legged brindle bull terrier. I liked Mrs Perkins straight away and the other two not quite so quickly. They showed us round the bungalow, and then said, 'We have to go out now. Will you be all right? Two ladies from next door will call in later to see if you need anything, and George will look after you, though he may want to be let out.' Daddy and they departed leaving me alone in a totally strange house, aged about fourteen, with only a very determined dog for company.

From their conversation Daddy discovered that my new foster parents were Christian Scientists and he asked them not to try to convert me, to which they were happy to agree. They kept their word, though I was intrigued to learn about their beliefs.

I had some supper and unpacked, when George made it clear that he wanted to go out by barking furiously, jumping up and down and rushing back and forth like a mad thing. So I let him out into the back garden and he shot out like a ball from a cannon, crashing through a cloche and breaking it into splinters, then on to the wood beyond the garden. It turned out that he had heard a fox and went in chase, but he never caught it. Actually he never managed to catch anything. Once, when out for a walk, he saw a large branch on a tree which he decided to pull down, but it was out of his reach. After much barking and leaping he caught it in his teeth but it would not come off. Despite much wriggling, growling and shaking it would not move, and we left him dangling from the tree. He arrived home late at night hungry and dishevelled.

The ladies from next door called, dressed for the drizzle that had set in, in plastic macs and pixie hoods. One was the owner of next door, Mrs Sylvia Gallatly, and the other was Lukie (to rhyme with 'spooky'), her companion. (There was also an elderly man living there called Uncle Jim who bred butterflies.) Sylvia's husband had owned Marshall and Snelgroves, a very posh shop in Oxford Street, but died when he fell in front of an Underground train early in the war. Their daughter Erica, a little younger than I, rarely appeared, since she was at boarding school. I went to bed and never even heard my new foster parents return from their evening out. The Perkinses had built the bungalow with their own hands when they were first married and over time had extended it, with furnishing entirely to my taste. Margaret had painted jolly patterns on the pelmets and on some of the furniture in the style of the Bloomsbury Group. Much classical music was played on records and I read all their Dickens books one after the other.

During the holidays Andrew, their only child, appeared home from his prep school and, although he was four or five years younger than I, we got on very well together. His best friends were the two sons of Barbara Brooke, the billeting officer, and their two sisters became in due course our bridesmaids, and Barbara godmother to Monica, our eldest daughter. Andrew was the same age as the younger brother and accompanied him to boxing lessons with Sergeant Buckle who also taught all of us youngsters swimming in a private pool in Ascot. I was not a good learner and soon lost what confidence I had.

Refugees had to report regularly to the police to establish their whereabouts with appropriate documents and this meant a journey to Ascot by bike for a photograph. The only studio there was labelled 'Alexander', and years later the photographer appeared at our wedding as Hugh's uncle.

I continued at the same school, Ranelagh, a co-educational grammar school, and was happy to have a shorter ride to reach it. At break-times we walked about in the grounds and were often joined by a little girl of four or so who lived in the house next door. She would bring her mug of 'national' (free and concentrated) orange juice with her and we watched transfixed as she waved her arms about while chatting vigorously: we expected her to spill it all over the place but she never did.

In the summer holidays the Brookes always organised a cricket match for their family and friends on the Ranelagh cricket pitch by kind permission of the headmaster, Mr Bury, who also played. I was useless at this and dreaded having to bat when he was bowling. He despatched me with his first ball and in my blind fury I put my tongue out at him.

To help with food-rationing people were encouraged to keep chickens in their gardens and the Perkinses and their neighbours, the Gallatlys, shared a large flock, taking it in turns, week on and week off, to feed them with a loathsome concoction of bought meal and food remnants including vegetable peelings. This gave off a nauseating smell while it was being cooked, stirred and distributed. I hated the chickens because they took up too much of Margaret's

Margaret's time which I would rather have had lavished on me, but having the eggs was admittedly a great help with the catering. Rationing also meant only two ounces of butter each per week; Margaret gave hers to Kenneth, 'the breadwinner'.

The radio was always on first thing in the morning for the news and later on for the day's household hints and recipes, one of these being parsnips mashed to resemble bananas. A second was making fudge out of condensed milk. All these were tried out. In another programme the Radio Doctor gave advice on keeping healthy (and the nation's health had never been better than under wartime conditions). Margaret and Kenneth, encouraged by the slogan 'Dig for Victory' gardened vigorously at the weekend raising vegetables and fruit; their delicious Alpine strawberries reminded me of the ones in Colfosco. They adored making bonfires but I did not like the smell, though many years later when Margaret came to stay with us she would find an excuse for a 'lovely bonfire', by which time I enjoyed them too.

Clothes being rationed, people used their ingenuity and skill to make skirts out of old curtains and underwear out of parachute material which was real silk, but usually with a camouflage pattern in khaki. Not very alluring. Margaret was very good at both dyeing and re-making old clothes so that grey flannel trousers turned into a dark red or blue lady's skirt. Barbara Brooke gave me an old blackout curtain, which I made into a beautiful swirly skirt decorated with braid round the hem. We produced handkerchiefs out of architect's tracing linen which had had its stiffening boiled

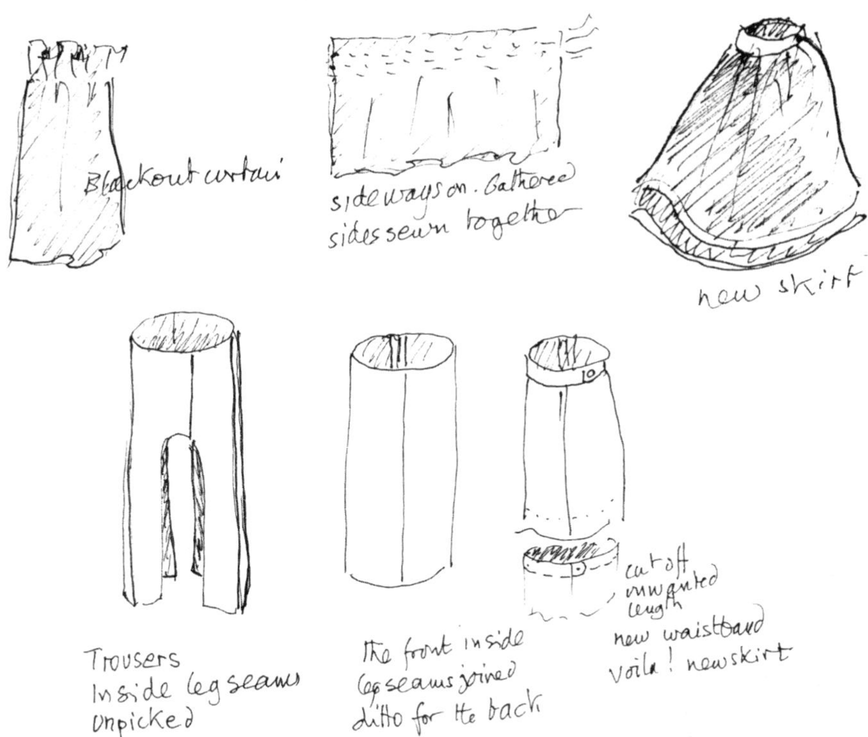

out, leaving the finest linen imaginable. I earned myself some pocket money by making soft toys for friends' children, which were not obtainable in shops, one of these being a lamb made out of an old white bath towel with unravelled black jumper for its legs and nose. We were for ever unravelling old woollies into hanks which were soaked in warm water and then hung on the line to dry and be straightened out, ready to be knitted up into another garment. Margaret was perpetually making jumpers for Andrew for which she needed no pattern, guessing the shape and size.

The Women's Institute, to which Margaret belonged, encouraged members to preserve surplus fruit by both bottling and canning. The former was common enough, but the latter was another matter. There were lessons in the art of canning and members took it in turn to borrow the necessary machine, though I never saw it in action. Not long after, there was an ear-splitting

Winding the wool from the old jumper

Winding the wrinkly wool into a skein.

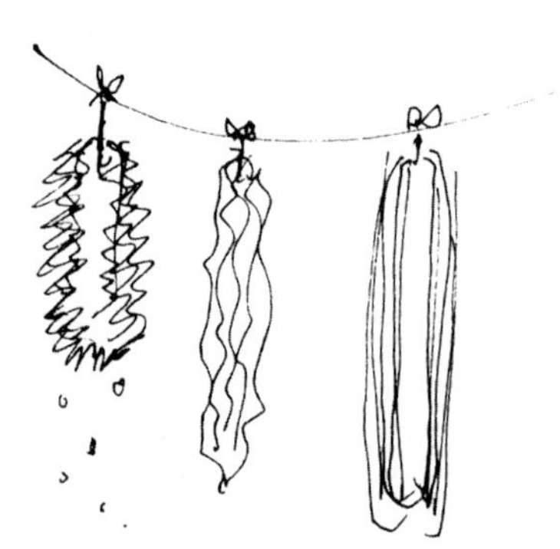

Stages in drying after a soak in warm water.

bang from inside the pantry and two of the cans had exploded. What a mess, and, what was worse, what a waste of precious fruit and sugar!

George, the bull terrier, was a great character. He arrived at the Perkinses' originally because Kenneth had bought him in London while under the influence. He was immensely strong both in body and in mind, barking and jumping up and down, all night long if necessary, until he had achieved his object or dropped from exhaustion. He once watched Margaret put the week's meat ration into the fridge and when she had gone into the garden to pick some parsley he attacked the fridge door with his teeth and claws until he had ripped it from its hinges; he had seized the joint and wolfed the meat by the time she returned. His punishment was a beating with a leather belt and all the strength that Kenneth could muster.

As George never managed to catch any creature we were surprised when he trotted in from one of his expeditions proudly carrying a rabbit in his mouth, which he laid at Margaret's feet as if to say, 'Now cook it for me'. Even before we were able to overcome our surprise there was a knock at the back door and a very cross gypsy woman confronted us, along with her white terrier. She said, 'Your dog made my dog drop the rabbit he had just caught and ran off with it', and demanded that we return it at once.

For my first Christmas at the Perkinses they kindly invited my parents from London, Tommy being in the army at this time. At bedtime Margaret showed them their room and asked, 'Is there anything else you need for the night?' Daddy replied, 'Just three things, please, - a hot water bottle, a thermos filled with hot water, and a bucket'. We did not know what to think or say or where to look. He quickly reassured us by explaining, 'The bucket is for emptying the hot water bottle into when it gets cold and the thermos is for refilling it.' We all

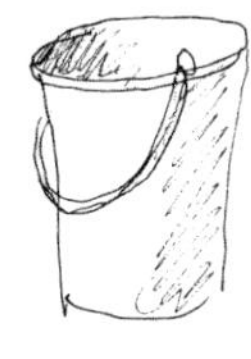

had a good laugh. He never minded people laughing at his efforts to achieve his own comfort.

He had an inventive turn of mind. On long train journeys he liked to sleep but because he found it very uncomfortable he devised long leather straps with buckles to fasten on to the luggage rack overhead to form loops in which he could rest his arms and his head. His travelling companions would sneer in derision but before long realised the benefits of this device. Knowing this he always carried a second pair to lend to an interested spectator.

When my mother developed multiple sclerosis he invented a one-legged stool to be strapped round her waist on which she could lean back to rest. Needless to say she refused to wear it, because she could not bear the thought of answering the door with this contraption sticking out behind her. To keep his trilby hat dry in the rain he devised a close-fitting cover made from waterproof material, securing it with paper clips round the edge of the brim. He did not stand on his dignity as long as he was comfortable.

My father always wore spats to keep his feet warm and dry. Fashionable in the 1920s, by 1940 they were a subject for ridicule. (The last pair for sale in London was in a Jermyn Street shop at the beginning of the war.) He strove hard to keep his in commission by means of paper clips, safety pins, glue and tape. The hardest part was to mend the elastic under the instep. After his death at the age of ninety-three, we offered them to the Museum of Costume in Manchester who received these rareties with delight.

Andrew and I were playing in my room one day and as I pushed him he tried to prevent himself from falling by grabbing the edge of the desk. To our amazement a secret drawer came out and fell on top of him on the floor. It disgorged a heap of sparkling jewels, necklaces, pearls, brooches, and gold and silver rings. The desk had belonged to Sylvia Gallatly next door who had sold it to Margaret, and was surprised and delighted to have these treasures returned to her because they were gifts to her as a bridesmaid at several weddings. As a reward she allowed me to choose one item for myself, a plaited gold bracelet in the shape of a snake with ruby eyes. This all seemed to me like a story in a *Girls' Own Annual.*

Our bungalow was hidden from the road by a small copse and it was here that Margaret undertook my first driving lesson in her Baby Austin. She showed me the controls and how to use them but I had not clearly understood the difference between the clutch being in and out. So we set off and before I had realised that we were moving we crashed into a birch tree. End of lesson; end of radiator; end of driving – for many years.

Down the road, in three linked railway carriages, lived Mr Samadini, a recluse with a French accent and a pock-marked complexion. In order to practise his herbal healing he had a couch for patients and shelves of potions. When I was taken there on an errand I found it very uncomfortable, not to say creepy.

Kenneth made early morning tea for Margaret in the kitchen where George slept, and as soon as the door was opened George would slip past and make straight for the marital bed and plunge headlong between the sheets ending up across Margaret's feet. There he would remain immovable, only extracting himself when he could no longer resist the smell of bacon cooking.

At Ranelagh the art lessons were terrible, taught by a nice old man but in a very antiquated way, with a wheel barrow or a pair of boots set up to be drawn with HB pencils on unsympathetic paper - enough to put anyone off art for life. I disliked gym because I was fearful about damaging myself climbing wall frames and vaulting over horses, not to mention handstands and, even worse, headstands. The only time I ever succeeded with a handstand was at a display performed by us girls for the boys of the next senior class. Taffy, the boy on whom I then had a crush, was going to be there, and it was imperative that I should not be labelled a wimp. By a vast effort of will-power I managed it, and the girl who had to catch my legs nearly fainted.

My maths was also hopeless, partly because I could see no adequate reason for learning it, but also because such a variety of schools and teachers had left me totally confused. The master kindly offered to give me some extra lessons after school, which I gladly accepted, but after a few weeks he gave me up as blocked beyond remedy. Eventually the School Certificate exams were over and one or two surprises lightened an otherwise dark scene, with passes in English, German, French and Art, so that the French mistress urged me to come back to do French in the sixth form, but I was aching to do dress design at art school. My father said that he could not afford this and from now on I had to contribute to my upkeep by taking a secretarial course.

Kenneth and Margaret, however, offered to finance a first year at the Art Department of Reading University and I went there in the autumn of 1944. I was deliriously happy, with many friends there and endless dances requiring floaty dresses. Margaret and others were generous in lending me some of their old ball gowns which we transformed into glorious creations by alterations of hems, removal of sleeves, or lowering of necklines. Professor Betts was in charge of the Art Department, a small, round man with dark hair and a pointed black beard. He attached great importance to life drawing, which he taught himself. I shall never forget my first life class. In the centre of the studio, full of students sitting at their 'donkeys' round a dais, stood a large, old, wrinkled lady stark naked posing for the class. I had seldom seen undressed people outside my home, and it took me some time to control my revulsion at this sight. (Wartime conditions had removed the beautiful, young and slim.) It was soon overcome as I struggled to draw this person, with unsatisfactory results, but the Professor saw signs of potential, and by the end of the year I had enough material to show at interviews for London art schools.

CHAPTER SEVEN

Back to London

In May 1945 the war in Europe ended, coinciding with the end of my year at Reading, and so I was able to return home to my parents in London, but I was torn between that happy thought and the sadness of leaving my foster parents of whom I had grown so fond. The first thing I remember about being back in the big city was V.E. night (for Victory in Europe) on May 10 when everyone in London seemed to converge by bus, train, Underground or on foot on Trafalgar Square, my parents and I included. There was singing, dancing and waving of flags. The crush was not to my liking, but everyone was friendly and well behaved. No more bombs, no more air raids; peace at last!

At home I looked for my childhood belongings from five years ago: where was the white dolls' pram, one of the few things that had come safely from Berlin? It had been given away. Where was the wooden cabinet that I had made with such loving care at my prep school and put in the attic? Fire precautions had required the removal of all inflammable material from attics in case of incendiary bombs, and so it was thrown out, unused. My mother showed me the inside of the big, built-in kitchen cupboard where all manner of things were kept, including old toys and newspapers, and now there was a huge black hole from the top through each shelf right down to the floor. An incendiary bomb had fallen through the roof and ceiling and had burned or charred all the contents. We still have a Monopoly board with a neat black-edged hole the size of the bomb in its middle. No doubt my father's training as an air-raid warden had helped to prevent the spread of the fire.

Like most teenagers (I was getting on for seventeen) I became disgruntled with my hair which had always been as straight as a die, and as a birthday present my parents gave me enough money to have a 'perm', entailing a hairdresser's appointment and then a very long sit in her chair, watching the process in the mirror. My hair was washed, dried and cut, and then a machine resembling a large black spider was wheeled behind me, its legs dangling down, each one then attached to a section of rolled-up hair encased in acrid smelling paper. The power was switched on, and I had to sit there feeling my head steadily heating up. I suddenly panicked, convinced that all may hair would be burned off, and wished that I had never been near the place. Eventually the spider was switched off, the curlers removed, the hair washed again then set in curlers with a perfumed lotion, and finally dried under a large dome. The tight curls were released and brushed to produce an effect worthy of Hollywood. I walked home self-consciously but vowed to myself 'never again'.

I had never been to the ballet and hoped that one day I would be invited by some gorgeous male in top hat and cloak when I could swan down a wide, curved staircase in a swirling dress to proceed with him to Covent Garden. In reality my first visit was on my own to a modest theatre at Swiss Cottage where I stood in the back of the stalls for the whole performance.

Kenneth rang me up from Bracknell one day, saying that he was coming up to town, and invited me to join him for dinner at the Normandy Hotel. I was thrilled to bits at this my first such invitation, especially with my new coiffure, and after the waiter had taken the order he remarked to

Kenneth, 'Your young lady is very pretty, sir.' Kenneth was livid at the implication, but I was rather flattered. Up till then the nearest I had been to eating out was at a British Restaurant, one of many set up and subsidised by the government for a nourishing meal without coupons for a shilling. Food at the Hampstead B.R. was just like home cooking because all the volunteer ladies were refugees from Europe and the atmosphere was more like a street party, with customers sitting on benches at trestle tables in church halls.

My parents once invited Mr and Mrs Lovett to tea with their son Martin, a handsome cello student with long slim fingers. He and his friends (who later became the Amadeus Quartet) used to practise in each other's houses, and one day in Ruth Bauer's basement I sat in while they practised Schubert's Trout Quintet. It was the first time I had been close to live music and to this day the Trout is one of my favourite pieces. I went out with Martin several times, but before long it was obvious that he had a more permanent acquisition, and one look from her made me beat a hasty retreat.

My father accompanied me with my portfolio to an interview with the Principal of St Martin's School of Art in Charing Cross Road where only recently a Dress Design course had been introduced, an innovation for Art Schools. I was enrolled for a four-year course, with a government grant, under Muriel Pemberton, a wonderful teacher, when one could catch her. She spent much time covering fashion shows in Paris for the *News Chronicle,* but came back full of the new trends and inspired us with her enthusiasm. Pam Swann taught us pattern cutting, but she also studied alongside us to obtain recognised qualifications. She had been a ballet dancer before the war, but her new husband, an R.A.F. pilot, was killed on the last day of the war, which meant that she had to earn her own living. During the course Pam asked me to assist her with one or two others in her own workroom in Baker Street making clothes for the theatre. This was a wonderful experience and had its exciting moments. One girl accidentally left a hot iron on a skirt about to be taken to the theatre. Panic ensued as we rushed round finding some matching material to mend the damage, and it was finally delivered in time. I also learned to pick up pins *en masse* at the end of the day with a magnet instead of picking each one up with my fingers as they dropped.

My good friend Anne de Lucovich, from the Fine Art Department, and I saved our bus fares by walking together the four or five miles from Primrose Hill, where I picked her up, through Regent's Park and down Tottenham Court Road to Charing Cross Road. With the money saved I bought myself a pair of ex-Land Army breeches because it had always been my dream to own riding breeches and a horse to match. I wore this garment on a visit to Bracknell and Kenneth was so uncomplimentary about my looks that I never put them on again.

I enjoyed all the work at St Martin's except, perhaps, the anatomy class because it was hard to learn the Latin names for all the muscles and draw them in their correct places. The master had an unkempt appearance but a friendly manner. It turned out that he lived alone in a flat with his beloved motor-bike under his bed. He was perpetually mending it, with the result that his finger-nails were always black, but apart from this he was a brilliant teacher and enabled all of us to pass our exams.

For relaxation there were dances galore, and at fancy-dress ones the Dress Design Department distinguished itself. A girl came to one of these in a sari which, being unprofessionally draped, so cocooned her legs that during one fox-trot she had to be lifted up and carried out like a corpse and unwound in the ladies room. There was a Dramatic Society where I took the part of the blind old father in *Tobias and the Angel*, but best of all were frequent visits to the National Gallery down the road, not only to study the pictures but also to listen to the lunch-time concerts given there under the direction of Dame Myra Hess. These had been started during the war to raise morale because of the air-raids, with distinguished musicians taking part including Leon Goossens with his oboe, Solomon the great pianist, and Kathleen Ferrier with her lovely contralto voice. Occasionally I bumped into Uncle Homi, my father's identical twin, giving lectures on restoration there to students. A friend of my father's was visiting the Gallery and passed a group with Homi bending forward to point out a detail. Thinking that he was my father he playfully pinched his bottom.

For the final exams we all made fabulous New Look clothes, from design to pattern-cutting and making up, some of which featured in an article with photographs in the *News Chronicle*. One girl designed such a complicated long white dress with a spiral black frill from neck to hem that it ran the risk of not being finished in time. So as soon as we had finished our own items we all set about helping her, and it was done.

At the end of the course an advertisement in *The Lady* enticed me to France, near Givet in the Ardennes, to look after two children of about five and six and teach them some English. An interview with their mother in London was successful and I went out there a week later for two months. Their large house accommodated Madame Viennôt (her husband, a diplomat in London, had died during the war), the two children, Rémi and Marianne, Germaine, the cook, and her husband Henri, and their little boy, Jacques. The path in front of the house ran beside the River Meuse, and behind was a large forest known for its snakes. Madame taught me how to inject anyone who had been bitten, but it was clear to me that I would never enter that wood on our daily walks. It stood on the frontier between France and Belgium, and two cousins of Rémi's and I were sent on a cycling expedition to Germaine's sister, over the border, to collect some provisions which were still rationed in France.

As soon as we arrived we were taken to a large table outside, groaning with delectable food including fruit tarts, each some eighteen inches across. After the first slice we were full, but it was clear that we were expected to have a slice of each variety. Fortunately there was a hungry dog under the table, who helped us

dispatch the surplus. Then loaded up with coffee, tea, sugar, butter, cheese and cereals, we returned with our booty through the dreaded forest. Germaine fed the Rice Crispies to the chickens, reckoning that such food was not fit for human beings. I would have given my bottom dollar for them, for they had been unobtainable in England.

Madame Viennôt had inherited several *châteaux*, but as she was a Socialist she gave most of them away to Socialist good causes. One of these, at Cabris in the south of France, became a study centre with a wonderful library in its tower. In its grounds she built two bungalows and a swimming pool for her children (which later we were lent for holidays with our children). Another, in Luxemburg, became an old people's home, where once we had lunch. The old folk leant back with their heads on Impressionist pictures, which I assumed to be prints, but Madame corrected me, assuring me that they were originals.

Around every bend in the grounds were life-size bronze statues, which turned out to be by Maillol.

After a few weeks in France I had amassed enough money to buy some material to make into a vast New Look coat for myself. At the market in Givet there was an amazingly full fabric stall, whereas in England there was no such choice available until many years later. The cloth I wanted caught my eye at once, typically French, a rather large black and white dog-tooth pattern. Back at the house I cut it out that night in my usual haste, though I eventually finished it back in London where it drew forth many complimentary comments. Not until three or four years later when living in Yorkshire did I discover that it was a traditional *English* fabric that had been exported to France.

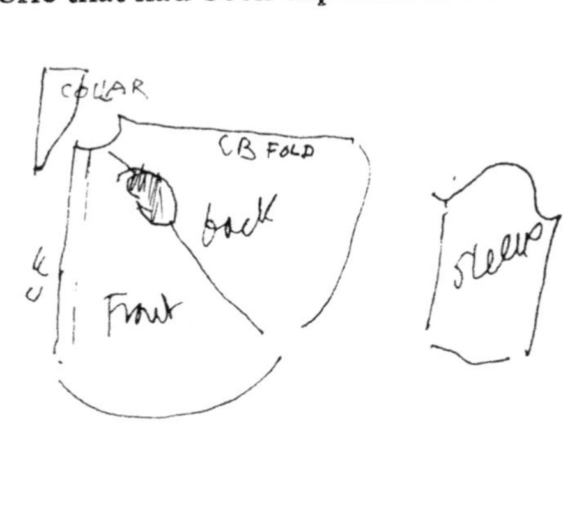

Towards the end of my stay Madame Viennôt, the cook and I with the three children, decamped to Paris where we stayed in Madame's large flat. The children were all whisked off to hospital to have their adenoids removed, and I was given *carte blanche* to explore Paris after a short induction course by Madame to the Lapin Agile (a famous café in Montmartre), the Eiffel Tower and the covered market, Les Halles. With my remaining pocket money I bought a terribly fetching navy suit with a pleated peplum at the back of the

jacket and a similarly pleated back to the straight skirt. I found an outsize Basque beret to complete my outfit, and this I wore for my 'going away' after our wedding. There was enough money left for a pair of nylon stockings, a very new invention, which in England had only been obtainable from America. These I laddered a few days later on the sharp corner of a baguette sticking out of my basket on the way home from the market.

On our return to Givet a letter from my father awaited me with the glad news that he had just received the naturalisation papers for all the family after a thirteen-year wait. I was beside myself with joy, able now to see the world no longer as a wandering German refugee but as a genuine British subject.

Afterwards

After qualifying as a dress designer (as my mother had done before me) I took an Art Teacher's course. This stood me in good stead when seeking part-time posts in Art Schools wherever my new husband's teaching and ,later, priestly work took us. In between the teaching we brought up three daughters.

My last post, at Keswick Hall College of Education in Norwich, led me to a turning point in my career when I was asked to design and make a cope for the Principal who was to be consecrated as Bishop of Bradwell (in Essex). Despite my dress-designing past I had never dreamt that I would spend the following thirty years making vestments for clergymen, and later clergy-women, and all manner of altar frontals, hangings, even banners and a triptych or two.

Eventually the inevitable eye-strain caused me to throw in the needle and take up water-colour painting, which has kept me enthralled for the last eight years.

It is perhaps not surprising that our daughters have inherited artistic traits. The eldest paints for pleasure; the middle one is a professional illustrator; and the youngest trained and practised as an art therapist. Several of the grandchildren show similar aptitudes. Is the clue perhaps in the genes?

R.M. 2004